Adaptation of Language Resources and Tools for Closely Related Languages and Language Variants 2013

AA004632

Associated with the 9th International Conference on Recent Advances in Natural Language Processing (RANLP 2013)

Hissar, Bulgaria
13 September 2013

ISBN: 978-1-62993-553-9

Printed from e-media with permission by:

Curran Associates, Inc.
57 Morehouse Lane
Red Hook, NY 12571

Some format issues inherent in the e-media version may also appear in this print version.

Copyright© (2013) by the Association for Computational Linguistics
All rights reserved.

Printed by Curran Associates, Inc. (2014)

For permission requests, please contact the Association for Computational Linguistics
at the address below.

Association for Computational Linguistics
209 N. Eighth Street
Stroudsburg, Pennsylvania 18360

Phone: 1-570-476-8006
Fax: 1-570-476-0860

acl@aclweb.org

Additional copies of this publication are available from:

Curran Associates, Inc.
57 Morehouse Lane
Red Hook, NY 12571 USA
Phone: 845-758-0400
Fax: 845-758-2634
Email: curran@proceedings.com
Web: www.proceedings.com

Preface

Recent initiatives in language technology have led to the development of at least minimal language processing kits for all official European languages. This is a big step towards automatic processing and/or extraction of information especially from official documents produced within the European Union. Apart from those official languages, a large number of dialects or closely related variants are in use, more and more not only as spoken colloquial languages but also in written media. Building language resources and tools is a cost-expensive operation and one can benefit form similarities among languages to reduce the effort in constructing LRs. One should be, however, aware also of the discrepancies which are often visible not only at the lexical level. Two examples could be different variants of Spanish in Latin America, German spoken in Austria and Switzerland, French – in France and Belgium, Dutch – in the Netherlands and Flemish in Belgium, etc. Less attention has been paid up to now to the development of LRs for such languages. This has a major impact on promoting language technology at the educational level, using information processing methods in all-day communication, social media, etc. This workshop intends to draw attention on issues mentioned above by bringing together scientists working with less resourced language variants and producing a roadmap of existing technologies and still existing gaps.

The current workshop aims to discuss topics like:

- Adaptation of monolingual tools for close languages and language variants;
- Case studies of using LRs and tools for standard languages on documents in language variants;
- Machine translation among closely related languages;
- Evaluation of LRs and tools for language variants and close languages;
- Linguistic issues in adaptation of LRs and tools (e.g. semantic discrepancies, lexical gaps, false friends);

We are very happy to include papers addressing topics not only from different language families (Germanic, Romance, Greek, Slavonic) but also going beyond the European borders (e.g. Rio de la Plata Spanish).

We hope that the current workshop will be an impulse for further activities related to the exploitation of language similarities for text technology. Finally, we would like to thank the organizers of the RANLP Conference for making the organization of this workshop possible and the programme committee for a fast and efficient reviewing process.

Cristina Vertan, Milena Slavcheva and Petya Osenova
Organisers of the Workshop on the Adaptation of Language Resources and Tools
for Closely Related Languages and Language Variants,
held in conjunction with the International Conference RANLP-13

Organizers:

Cristina Vertan (University of Hamburg)
Milena Slavcheva (IICT, Bulgarian Academy of Sciences)
Petya Osenova (Sofia University "St. Kl. Ohridski" and IICT, Bulgarian Academy of Sciences)

Program Committee:

Laura Alonso y Alemany (Univeristy of Cordoba, Argentina)
César Antonio Aguilar (Pontificia Universidad Católica de Chile, Sntiago de Chile, Chile)
Antonio Branco (University of Lisabon)
Gerhard Budin (University of Vienna, Austria)
Jose Castaño (University of Buenos Aires, Argentina)
Walter Daelemans (University of Antwerp, Belgium)
Tomaz Erjavec (Jozef Stefan Institute, Slovenia)
Maria Gavrilidou (ILSP, Greece)
Walther v. Hahn (University of Hamburg,Germany)
Susane Jekat (ZHAW, Winterthur, Switzerland)
Cvetana Krstev (University of Belgrade, Serbia)
Vladislav Kuboň (Charles University Prague, Czech Republic)
John Nerbone (University of Gröningen, the Netherlands)
Maciej Ogrodniczuk (IPAN, Polish Academy of Sciences)
Petya Osenova (University of Sofia, Bulgaria)
Stelios Piperidis (ILSP, Greece)
Laurent Romary (INRIA, France)
Kiril Simov (Bulgarian Academy of Sciences)
Milena Slavcheva (Bulgarian Academy of Sciences)
Daniel Stein (University of Hamburg, Germany)
Marco Tadić (University of Zagreb, Croatia)
Cristina Vertan (University of Hamburg)
Duško Vitas (University of Belgrade, Serbia)
Kalliopi Zervanou (University of Tilburg, the Netherlands)

Table of Contents

Conference Program

13.09.2013

(9:15 - 10:15) Invited Talk

Combining, Adapting and Reusing Bi-texts between Related Languages: Application to Statistical Machine Translation (invited talk)
Preslav Nakov

Session 1: Machine Translation

(10:15 - 10:45)

Language diversity and implications for Language technology in the Multilingual Europe
Cristina Vertan and Walther von Hahn

(11:15 - 11:45)

Corpus development for machine translation between standard and dialectal varieties
Barry Haddow, Adolfo Hernandez, Friedrich Neubarth and Harald Trost

(11:45 - 12:15)

Adaptation of a Rule-Based Translator to Río de la Plata Spanish
Ernesto López, Luis Chiruzzo and Dina Wonsever

Session 2: Language processing

(13:30 - 14:00)

Text segmentation for Language Identification in Greek Forums
Pavlina Fragkou

(14:00 - 14:30)

Lexicon induction and part-of-speech tagging of non-resourced languages without any bilingual resources
Yves Scherrer and Benoît Sagot

(14:30 - 15:00)

The Mysterious Letter J
Andjelka Zecevic and Stasa Vujicic-Stankovic

Combining, Adapting and Reusing Bi-texts between Related Languages: Application to Statistical Machine Translation (invited talk)

Preslav Nakov
Qatar Computing Research Institute
Tornado Tower, floor 10, PO box 5825
Doha, Qatar
pnakov@qf.org.qa

1 Abstract

Bilingual sentence-aligned parallel corpora, or *bi-texts*, are a useful resource for solving many computational linguistics problems including part-of-speech tagging, syntactic parsing, named entity recognition, word sense disambiguation, sentiment analysis, etc.; they are also a critical resource for some real-world applications such as statistical machine translation (SMT) and cross-language information retrieval. Unfortunately, building large bi-texts is hard, and thus most of the 6,500+ world languages remain resource-poor in bi-texts. However, many resource-poor languages are related to some resource-rich language, with whom they overlap in vocabulary and share cognates, which offers opportunities for using their bi-texts.

We explore various options for bi-text reuse: (i) direct combination of bi-texts, (ii) combination of models trained on such bi-texts, and (iii) a sophisticated combination of (i) and (ii).

We further explore the idea of generating bi-texts for a resource-poor language by adapting a bi-text for a resource-rich language. We build a lattice of adaptation options for each word and phrase, and we then decode it using a language model for the resource-poor language. We compare word- and phrase-level adaptation, and we further make use of cross-language morphology. For the adaptation, we experiment with (a) a standard phrase-based SMT decoder, and (b) a specialized beam-search adaptation decoder.

Finally, we observe that for closely-related languages, many of the differences are at the subword level. Thus, we explore the idea of reducing translation to character-level transliteration. We further demonstrate the potential of combining word- and character-level models.

2 Author's Biography

Dr. Preslav Nakov is a Scientist in the Arabic Language Technologies group at the Qatar Computing Research Institute (QCRI), Qatar Foundation. His research interests include computational linguistics, machine translation, lexical semantics, Web as a corpus, and biomedical text processing. His current research focus is on Arabic language processing, with an emphasis on statistical machine translation to/from Arabic.

Before joining QCRI, Dr. Nakov was at the National University of Singapore, where he worked on text and spoken language machine translation for Asian languages, including Chinese, Malay and Indonesian. Prior to that, he was at the Bulgarian Academy of Sciences and the Sofia University, where he was an honorary lecturer. He received his Ph.D. in Computer Science from the University of California at Berkeley in 2007, supported by a Fulbright grant and a Berkeley fellowship.

Dr. Nakov authored three books, one book chapter, and many research papers at conferences such as ACL, HLT-NAACL, EMNLP, ICML, CoNLL, COLING, EACL, ECAI, and RANLP, and journals such as JAIR, TSLP, NLE and LRE. He received the Young Researcher Award at RANLP'2011. He was also the first to receive the Bulgarian President's John Atanasoff annual award for achievements in the development of the information society (December 2003); the award is named after an American of Bulgarian ancestry who co-invented the first automatic electronic digital computer, the Atanasoff-Berry computer.

Dr. Nakov has served on the program committee of the major conferences and workshops in computational linguistics, including as a co-organizer and an area/publication/tutorial chair.

Language diversity and implications for Language technology in the Multilingual Europe

Cristina Vertan
University of Hamburg
cristina.vertan@uni-hamburg.de

Walther v. Hahn
University of Hamburg
vhahn@informatik.uni-hamburg.de

Europe has a particular and unique setting. On one had it has a great language diversity, there are twenty four official languages and a dozen of minority languages largely used. On the other hand most of these languages belong to one of the indo-European language families (Roman, Germanic Slavic) and within these language families similarities at lexical and syntactic level can be observed. Whilst an increased attention have been given to the development of language technology tools for the official EU –Languages, processing tools for minority languages have a chance to progress only by exploiting similarities within their language families.

In order to have an overview about the European linguistic diversity and the implications on the language technology research we republish here a part of the article

"Translation Difficulties and Information Processing Problems with Eastern European Languages"

Cristina Vertan and Walther v.Hahn

Published din the volume "Multilingual Processing in Eastern and Southern EU Languages", Cambridge Scholar Press, 2012

It is still popular today to blame machine translation (MT) for poor translations of literary texts. However, even inelegant translations are an industrial factor in producing MT software, in selling multilingual retrieval for relevance scanning or in opening markets by issuing simple foreign-language descriptions. Information retrieval (IR) technologies are effective even if their degree of linguistic correctness is low.
The success story of Machine Translation is partly owed to some simplifications, which made its start-up easier (leaving aside the political presetting of English-Russian translations). Simplifying reality was a promising approach, because the reduction of parameters from syntax, morphology, and domain coverage formed the basis for the demonstration of MT's feasibility.
Moreover, the statistical approach in MT nourished the hope that reasonable results for English can be seen as evidence for the fact that MT can be done with similar quality for any other language.
In subsequent decades experiments were performed with numerous other language pairs around the world including languages even, for which detailed linguistic knowledge was unavailable . The goal of these scientific and industrial research efforts was mainly to estimate the quality and costs of acceptable MT products for the commercially meaningful language pairs. The same holds true for multilingual information retrieval and multilingual information processing on other fields.
With the ever growing number of language pairs for which customers require cost-efficient processing, four aspects became clear:

1. There are domains and language pairs for which not even human translation/IR is available, e.g., financial law texts from Finish to, say, Hausa. The question remains how to obtain these at all.
2. There is no representative bilingual data collection (a "corpus") for these language pairs at all. Statistical approaches hence will not be feasible within the next 5-10 years. How to obtain inexpensive translations in the mid-term for these "low resourced" languages?
3. Many languages (e.g., Hausa) have more than one writing system or changing orthography (compare the post-reform rules for German orthogography that are in force since 2006). This poses the challenge of how to obtain homogeneous corpora.
4. Multinational or global companies need language processing for promotion, local instruction, or contracts, that affords legally binding results.

The optimism of the pioneering years has yielded to scepticism regarding general recipes for multilingual processing such as translation, even for the traditional Western languages. In Europe, the expansion of the EU additionally demonstrated that democratic co-operation requires a huge work load of translation and bilingual information processing among today's 23 official languages. The sheer number of languages, their diverse linguistic structure and their different public use are reasons enough to give up some of the starting assumptions and simplifications of the first decades.
We discusses the rather different situations in Europe with regards to cross-lingual processing tasks in an English and American context along the following dimensions:

1 Languages

There are 230 spoken languages in Europe. Most of them have a long common history in the Indo-European paradigm. Even among the 23 official languages of the EU there are the Finno-Ugric official languages Finnish, Estonian and Hungarian. The Turkic and Mongolic families also have several European members, while the north Caucasian and Kartvelian families are important in the south-eastern border of geographical Europe. The Basque language of the Western Pyrenees is an isolated language, unrelated to any other language group in Europe. Much less known even to Central European citizens is the existence of a European Semitic language, the Maltese, written in Latin letters.
In the current volume we decided to refer only to the official EU languages, as representatives of most of the families enumerated above. Additionally, due to European integration there is an increased need in translation and cross-lingual management of documents in these languages. We hope that the some solutions presented here can be applicable also for non-official and minority languages of the EU.
Even the simple enumeration of the language families encountered in Europe already reveals the existence of major graphemic, phonetic and structural differences amongst them. The aim of this volume is not to investigate these differences from a linguistic point of view, but rather to insist on those discrepancies that trigger challenges for any translation system or cross-lingual/multilingual application. In this sense the following aspects are of relevance:

1.1 Writing differences

Although Europe has no unusual iconographic or syllabic writing systems but only phonographic paradigms, there are nevertheless problems with gathering homogenous bilingual language resources, i.e., training material for statistical approaches.

Cyrillic transliterations for named entities (NEs) follow four different (target language independent) transliteration schemata and numerous (target language dependent) transcriptions. As an example, consider the (operating system dependent) specific encodings for Bulgarian Cyrillics in contrast to Russian encoding. A similar situation exists for Arabic NEs in Maltese. The transliteration is not always standardised, which often leads to data sparseness. One word transliterated in three different ways will be identified in fact as three different words. Moreover, there is a problem with older electronic resources that were developed before the introduction of the Unicode character set: Many languages adopted transliteration simplifications that induce undesired ambiguities. For example the Romanian word for "goose" contains two diacritics "gâscă". A corpus collected before the introduction of the Unicode system would simplify this word to "gasca", which may be read also as "gașcă" denoting a group of young people.

1.2 Variety of Linguistic Structure

European languages differ centrally in their use of pronouns and articles. So called "pro-drop" languages like Italian do not express the 1st person sg. pronouns explicitly, but mark them morphologically, whereas non-pro-drop languages like German have to add the pronoun explicitly in examples like "Ich gehe zu ihm" (I am going to him). Even more difficult in this sense is Hungarian, where lots of particles are only attached as morphemes (összerakhatatlanságukért = "for their quality of not being easy to put together")[1].
Grammatical gender is present or not (English, Basque), is expressed in noun endings (Italian, mostly), or not (German, mostly), affects other words by agreement (Spanish, French) affects the demonstratives (Italian), or not (Greek), is additionally marked by articles (German, but not

[1] This example is owed to Merényi Csaba from MorphoLogic

unambiguously), or not (Bulgarian, the Baltic languages). Articles are in use for the three-gender system (German), or two genders (Maltese), or the middle (Romanian, common singular for masc. and ntr.) attached to the end of a word (Romanian), or separated in front of the noun (French). Moreover, grammatical and natural gender have an unclear relation in most languages.

All these are major challenges especially in machine translation (MT) whenever the target language is more productive in pronouns or articles than the source. Rule based MT needs a deep linguistic analysis module and often the involvement of large knowledge bases in order to infer the correct target pronoun, while corpus-based MT cannot cope with this problem at all. In most cases the translation lacks not only the correct pronoun but also all derived information such as the correct inflection of the dependent nouns, adjectives and verbs.

To express definiteness, some languages use articles, while others express it by word order, which normally gets lost in surface-form statistical MT systems.

The word order of adjective and noun is semantically relevant in Spanish, restricted in German and fixed in English. Also the position of a verb in the sentence varies among language families. This is a real challenge not only for translation systems but also for multilingual tools that try to apply the same analysis technique to several structurally different languages. Rule-based tools lack a substantial number of common rules. Statistical methods, on the ther hand, require the availabilty of huge non-sparse data covering all these phenomena.

Word composition plays a major role in many EU languages and the order of components is significant. Sometimes logical particles must be inserted for correct translation. Distant verb particles in German are very difficult to differentiate from prepositions when only statistical methods are being applied. Again, such particularities constitute challenges not only in translation but for any preprocessing step in cross-linguistic processing.

1.3 Contact

All these languages have been in extensive contact with each other over time with the result, that additional irregularities were introduced. In Romanian, for example, one third of the vocabulary stems from Russian, Hungarian and German and has only been assimilated superficially. This means that the graphemic rules for Romanian are not homogenous. The contact, however, differs from language to language. Compare Romanian-Italian and Slovene-Italian contacts, e.g. whichdiffer with respect to the historical time, when the contact was established. Italy influenced Slovenia much more through Venetian than through modern Italian.

Borrowings were often done only partially so not all semantics is preserved. A special situation is encountered on the Balkan Peninsula where vocabulary related to food, e.g., old weapons or customs are usually shared by neighbouring communities but not necessarily by whole countries. For example, a lot of regional words in the North-Western part of Romania (Transylvania) are in common with Hungarian and German, but unknown in the Southern part of the country, which otherwise uses more words shared with Turkish and Bulgarian.

This constitutes a real challenge for modern retrieval systems which make use of ontologies. Building a language-independent ontology is an extremely difficult task, and even word-based semantic networks are highly problematic. A series of papers published over the last years report the difficulties in adapting the English Word-Net to each of the Balkan languages, and the challenge of homogenisation amongst these Word-Nets.

These considerations, however, touch upon cultural differences, that are addressed in the following paragraphs of this paper. We demonstrate with a few observations that behind the language differences in the EU there are many more cultural differences than between two regions of one country.

2 Text Structures, Forms and Formats

Two textual peculiarities of European publications are very confusing in corpora:

European texts often quote passages in a foreign language such as English or other European languages, because of a close contact with that language. Translated quotations from web pages, hence, are not always in the correct language, as an MT tool has been used.

A typical text form for an application, for an objection, for an expertise etc. differs not only lexically but also in style and form between European countries.

3 Cultures of Textuality

In Europe the influence of English varies from country to country. A comparison of German and French shows that an official inhibitive language policy influenced the borrowings to a high degree in France. Looking to Hungarian one can observe that the French policy more or less succeeded in most technical fields, whereas in Hungary two different medical nomenclatures exist that in practice and international information exchange conflict severely.

Irrespectively of a country's official language policy, the language policy of companies is also changing dramatically. A recent study observed that in Germany slightly more than 50% of all companies use German as the only business language, another 20% use German and English or only English, respectively. Less than 4% use other languages.

In general, technical fields in countries have a different degree of textualisation dependent on technologies, which have a higher or lower distance to text production and use, e.g. carpet weaving, vs. violin making vs. ecological food supplier vs. photo-copying or services.

Correspondingly, the reference to computerised texts, e.g. interactive web forms or download resources of public service differs very much between European countries, say, between Finland and Poland. While web forms must be explained even for language minorities, paper forms are issued by offices, where misunderstandings may be resolved in direct contact.

4 Commercial Market Value

The possible market value of multilingual or cross-lingual technologies clearly depends on the mere number of publications accessible and resulting from trade and industry. If you compare a Slavonic language minority like the Sorbs in Germany to Polish speakers in Poland, it becomes clear that the industrial expansion in Poland and exports abroad result in a disproportionately more extensive language and information contact than that for Sorbian speakers. Translating a handbook of nano technology into Polish makes more sense than translating it into Sorbian or publishing Shakespeare's works in Frisian, another German minority language.

5 Background and Perspectives

To come back to the main issue: Language technology in Europe is not an extension of known technologies to new languages, but a multidimensional challenge for science, technology and politics of quite another order of magnitude. It will bind research groups, translators, software companies and politicians for the next 50 years at least.

There is a widespread conception that

- the rapid development of the Internet,
- with new web services,
- the globalisation of the markets and
- the increase of online transactions

are the main factors driving international research in language technology.

This argument is, at least in a European context, only partially valid. In the era when Internet was in its infancy, and most part of the online information was exclusively distributed in English, the Directorate General of EU "Linguistic Applications" was already concerned with the additional languages from the countries willing to join the European Union.

"With the expected enlargement of the EU following the accession of up to ten Central and Eastern European countries (referred to as CEECs, which is the usual EU abbreviation), the translation complexity takes a quantum leap. The current EU languages (n.R. situation in 1998) (Danish, Dutch, English, Finnish, French, German, Greek, Italian, Portuguese, Spanish and Swedish) can be translated in 110 language combinations, as each of the 11 languages can be translated into 10 other languages. With the addition of 10 new languages (Estonian, Latvian, Lithuanian, Polish, Czech, Slovak, Hungarian, Slovenian, Romanian and Bulgarian) the complexity goes up to 21 x 20 = 420 language combinations, but there is no obvious political or linguistic justification for changing the European Union's official policy of supporting multilingualism, which finds its expression in the MLIS programme, among others."

(Poul Andersen, DG XIII EU Representative, in an article "Translation Tools for the CEEC Candidates for EU Membership - an Overview", *Terminologie et Traduction* 1.1998, pp.140-166).

One can only speculate about the development in Europe in multilingual language technology without the political changes of 1989. The rule-based machine translation system Systran was functional, with reasonable performance for the EU-languages and for the requirements of that time, namely translation of easy official documents.

We assume that the dramatic development of multilingual language technology in Europe was in fact driven by two forces: The new political context and the social impact of the Internet, rather than the economy.

We are also convinced that the European approach to multilingual language technology gave an impulse all around the globe to develop applications for various language communities: Recently systems for several Ethiopian languages appeared, a machine translation system for Quechua was presented (to quote only a few examples).

.

Corpus development for machine translation between standard and dialectal varieties

Barry Haddow[1], Adolfo Hernández Huerta[2], Friedrich Neubarth[2], Harald Trost[3]

[1)] ILCC, School of Informatics, University of Edinburgh
bhaddow@staffmail.ed.ac.uk

[2)] Austrian Research Institute f. Artificial Intelligence (OFAI)
{adolfo.hernandez, friedrich.neubarth}@ofai.at

[3)] Institute for Artificial Intelligence, Medical University of Vienna
harald.trost@meduniwien.ac.at

Abstract

In this paper we describe the construction of a parallel corpus between the standard and a non-standard language variety, specifically standard Austrian German and Viennese dialect. The resulting parallel corpus is used for statistical machine translation (SMT) from the standard to the non-standard variety. The main challenges to our task are data scarcity and the lack of an authoritative orthography. We started with the generation of a base corpus of manually transcribed and translated data from spoken text encoded in a specifically developed orthography. This data is used to train a first phrase-based SMT. To deal with out-of-vocabulary items we exploit the strong proximity between source and target variety with a backoff strategy that uses character-level models. To arrive at the necessary size for a corpus to be used for SMT, we employ a boot-strapping approach. Integrating additional available sources (comparable corpora, such as Wikipedia) necessitates to identify parallel sentences out of substantially differing parallel documents. As an additional task, the spelling of the texts has to be transformed into the above mentioned orthography of the target variety.

1 Introduction

Statistical machine translation between dialectal varieties and their cognate standard variety is a challenge quite different from translation between major languages with large resources on both sides. Instead of having huge corpora at hand that offer themselves for machine learning techniques, substantial written corpora of dialectal language varieties are rare. In addition, there is no authoritative orthography, which calls for methods to normalize the spelling of existing written texts. Parallel resources for a standard language and a dialectal variety thereof are even less common. But such parallel data is the workhorse of modern machine translation systems and key to producing sufficiently natural utterances. On the positive side, the relative proximity between a standard language and its varieties opens up new possibilities to gather parallel data, despite data sparsity.

In this paper we will outline methods to acquire such data, developed for a specific pair of varieties, Austrian German (AG), the standard variety, and a dialectal variety spoken in the capital, Viennese dialect (VD) (Schikola, 1954), (Hornung, 1998).[1] From a linguistic perspective, it has to be noted that dialects generally are not really homogenous. Lacking standardization initiatives, reinforcement by education or public media and predominantly being confined to oral usage, dialects most often form a dynamic continuum between different varieties and speaker groups. Being defined by social group rather than geographical regions, the Viennese variety is a sociolect in the strict sense, where dialects in urban regions are generally associated with lower social classes (Labov, 2001). Also, speakers with native competence usually adapt the register to the communicative situation as well as to the content of the utterances in a very dynamic way. Switching between varieties and subtle gradual shifts are a very natural phenomenon in such a linguistic situation.

While being aware that the linguistic conception of a dialect is not uncontroversial, we still think that it is feasible and appropriate to model a dialectal variety that conforms to a stereotype of that dialect.

The paper focuses on the generation of the resources necessary for statistical machine translation between a standard variety with rich resources (AG) and a dialectal variety (VD) with almost no resources. The strategy is to create a minimal base corpus comprising bilingual data in a standardized orthography for VD, and in a second step applying a bootstrapping strategy in order to gain a suf-

[1]The work presented in this paper is based on the project 'Machine Learning Techniques for Modeling of Language Varieties' (MLT4MLV - ICT10-049) funded by the Vienna Science and Technology Fund (WWTF).

ficient amount of bilingual lexical resources and to increase the data on the basis of automatically generated translations. As proximity between the varieties works on our side, we give detailed descriptions of how the linguistic closeness can be exploited to bootstrap the required resources.

2 Background

Pairs of closely related languages (or language varieties) offer themselves to exploit the linguistic proximity in order to overcome the usual scarcity of parallel data. Nakov and Tiedemann (2012) take advantage of the great overlap in vocabulary and the strong syntactic and lexical similarity between Bulgarian and Macedonian. They develop an SMT system for this language pair by employing a combination of character and word level translation models, outperforming a phrase-based word-level baseline. Regarding MT of dialects, Zbib et al. (2012) use crowdsourcing to build Levantine-English and Egyptian-English parallel corpora; while Sawaf (2010) normalizes non-standard, spontaneous and dialect Arabic into Modern Standard Arabic to achieve translations into English.

A considerable amount of work has been done on extracting parallel sentences from comparable corpora, i.e. a set of documents in different languages that contains similar information. Munteanu and Marcu (2005) use a Maximum Entropy classifier trained on parallel sentences to determine if a sentence pair is parallel or not. Based on techniques of Information Retrieval, Abdul-Rauf and Schwenk (2011) use the translations of a SMT system in order to find the corresponding parallel sentences from the target-language side of the comparable corpus. Smith et al. (2010) explore Wikipedia to extract parallel sentences where, once they achieve an alignment at the document level by taking advantage of the structure of this online encyclopedia, they train Conditional Random Fields to tackle the task of sentence alignment. Tillmann and Xu (2009) extract sentence pairs by a model based on the IBM Model-1 (Brown et al., 1993) and perform training on parallel data. With the exception of Munteanu and Marcu (2005), where bootstrapping techniques find application, these methods require (and presuppose the existence of) a certain amount of resources (i.e. parallel data or lexicon coverage) not available for some languages or varieties.

3 Constructing a Parallel Corpus

For Standard German to Viennese dialect, there were no existing parallel data sets and, moreover, most monolingual text sources that exist are written in an inconsistent way, oscillating between standard conventions and free attempts to encode the phonetic realization in the dialect. The first step was to design an orthographic standard for the target language that would be consistent, unambiguous and phonologically transparent. In the light of applicability in language technology, accuracy towards phonological properties seemed the most important criterion, on a par with the necessity to minimize lexical ambiguities. This is different from producing literary texts, where readability might be a more prominent issue, and the orientation towards the standard orthography may have a higher priority.

A second problem with initial data acquisition is the fact that dialect speakers in Vienna very often switch between the dialect and the standard variety, depending on the communicative situation, but also on the content that may invite to use a higher register. Text data with a bias towards the standard by virtue of standard orthography quite often also reflects such switching processes. In order to circumvent such biases, we carefully selected colloquial data of VD that are as authentic to the dialect as possible. The basic material consists of transcripts of TV documentaries and free interview recordings of dialect speakers. The transcripts were manually translated into both AG and VD, the latter being vacuous in most cases. This way we could ensure that (rarely occurring) switchings into the standard would not end up in the target model. A typical example looks as follows, where AG and VD refer to the standard and the Viennese orthography of a sentence from our corpus.

(1) AG: `Ja, ich weiß es doch.`
VD: `Jå, i waas s e.`
'yes, I know it anyway.'

In an early stage, we were interested in finding a way to align these parallel sentences on a word-by-word basis, in order to simultaneously generate lexical resources comprising morphology and morpho-syntactic features (PoS tags, grammatical features, such as gender, case, person, number etc.). Given that usually the two translations are syntactically very similar, with little reordering and/or n-to-n correspondences, and also that many corresponding words are 'cognates', meaning that they are lexically (and morphologically) the same in both varieties, with different phonology and spelling (e.g., AG *'weiß'* corresponds to VD *'waas'* "(I) know"), we bootstrapped a word-alignment routine that very soon provided promising results.

The core idea was to use the string edit distance (Levenshtein algorithm) to determine whether two words should be aligned or not. Because it matters if one or more editing steps (errors) occur in a short or in a long word, we normalized the string edit distance by a factor consisting of the logarithm of the average string length or a special penalty factor for very short strings). However, the orthographic forms may differ substantially while referring to identical words. So, the second ingredient was to train a character based translation model between AG and VD, using the data-driven grapheme-to-phoneme converter Sequitur G2P (Bisani and Ney, 2008). These automatically generated strings of dialect words (VD*) are then compared to the words of the target (VD). Given that the initial data is very limited, the results of the G2P translation are not reliable as a translation, but still very useful to determine the distance measure. Since the full set of extracted word pairs (after validation) is used to re-train the models in an iterative way, the word alignment gets better the more data is added. In a way, over-fitting, generally carefully avoided in statistical modeling, works to our advantage.

The alignment algorithm in a first step linearly searches for the best path of matches. If the score provided by the string edit distance is above a given threshold, insertions and deletions are the less costly options, and the words will not be aligned. By this method, we would only align cognates and miss the more interesting cases where words of AG are translated into different words that may be typical for the dialect (e.g., VD has a special word for AG *'Polizist'* "policeman": VD *'kibara'*). Therefore two more iterations over the set of aligned pairs try to find these non-cognate pairs. First, adjacent insertions and deletions are aligned regardless of the distance measure. This guarantees that word pairs that are not cognates (with a high degree of similarity), but different lexical items, are also captured by the word alignment, given that the syntactic structure of the source and the target sentence are approximately the same. Second, non-adjacent insertion-deletion pairs with a distance measure below the threshold are marked as valid alignments. That way the algorithm that by itself provides only linear alignments is also capable to capture some non-local alignments resulting from syntactic re-ordering.

With regard to SMT and contemplating the immanent problem of data sparsity, it seems obvious that a factorized translation model (Koehn and Hoang, 2007) will have certain advantages over a translation model that only considers full word forms. This, however, requires the generation of lexical resources for both language varieties. For the source language (AG) such resources already exist. The question is, if and how the lexical information stemming from the source language can be transferred onto the target language.

Our word alignment is capable of identifying cognates. However, these cognates will only cover certain word forms out of more complex morphological paradigms. Given that for AG, the lemma and the information about the paradigm can be automatically retrieved from the word form, the task is to identify lemma and the paradigm from the VD word form. In many cases it will suffice to strip off the inflectional endings and to transfer the morphological information from the AG entry. However, there are many deviations (from AG to VD) as well as exceptions, also only real cognates can be treated that way, so there has to be done some manual validation in order to create a VD lexicon that in the end covers all word forms.

(2)	INPUT:	`haus`	`NN Neut . -I-a`
	OUTPUT:	haus	haus+NN+Neut+Sg+NDA
		heisa	haus+NN+Neut+Pl+NDA

sg./pl. forms of VD 'haus' (AG 'Haus' *'house'*)

When the lemma, the major category and the relevant morphological information are identified, this is sufficient to generate all word forms together with morphological features in a given language variety.

4 Machine Translation Experiments

In this section we report on some experiments using the data set described in the previous section to build statistical machine translation systems, using Moses (Koehn et al., 2007).

4.1 Corpus

The corpus was split into four sections, TRAIN, DEV, DEVTEST and TEST, where the first was used for estimation of phrase tables and language models, the second for tuning the MT system parameters and the third for testing during system development. The last was reserved for final testing. The relative sizes of the three section is shown in Table 1.

Section	Sentences	Tokens	
		AG	VD
TRAIN	4909	39108	40031
DEV	600	4775	4882
DEVTEST	600	4712	4803
TEST	600	4841	4943

Table 1: Corpus sizes (untokenised)

4.2 Word-level Models

The word-level models are standard phrase-based models built using Moses. The parallel text is tokenised using the Moses tokeniser for German, then it is all lowercased. This parallel text is then aligned in both directions using GIZA++ (Och and Ney, 2000) and the alignments are symmetrised using the "grow-diag-final-and" heuristic. The aligned parallel text is then used to estimate a translation table using the standard Moses heuristics, and a 3-gram language model built on the target side of the parallel text using SRILM with Kneser-Ney smoothing. The translation and language models are then combined with a distance-based reordering model and their weights optimised for BLEU using MERT on the DEV corpus.

4.3 Character-level Models

In earlier work on MT for closely-related languages (Vilar et al., 2007; Tiedemann, 2009; Nakov and Tiedemann, 2012), it has been shown that character-level translation models can be effective. These character-level models are also built using phrase-based Moses, but allowing it to treat single characters or groups of characters as "tokens". In the unigram character-level model, we treat each character as a separate token by inserting a space between each of them, and using a special character (||) to indicate word boundaries. For the bigram character-level model, the "tokens" are pairs of adjacent characters, with the same word boundary character as in the unigram model. Table 1 shows examples of a German sentence converted into suitable formats for the character-level unigram and bigram models.

After decoding with one of the character-level models, converting back to word-level text is straightforward in the unigram case; it is just a matter of removing spaces then replacing the special word-boundary character with a space. For the bigram-level model, we remove the first character in each bigram then proceed as for the unigram-level models.

Other than the word-to-character conversion of all data, the character-based models are trained using the standard Moses training pipeline. We use the default maximum phrase-length of 7, and a 7-gram language model, parameters that were observed to work best in early experiments. During tuning, we maximise word-level BLEU with respect to the reference.

4.4 Backoff Models

After observing the performance of word and character-level models, we decided to try to combine them into a *backoff* model, which would use the word-level translation wherever possible, but apply the character-level model for unknown words. In (Nakov and Tiedemann, 2012), they found that a similar model combination gave the best results when translating between closely related languages.

Firstly, we experimented with different variations of the character-level model for the unknown words (OOVs). Each of these models is trained and tuned on the TRAIN and DEV sets, and we report accuracies on the OOVs in DEVTEST (OOV according to the phrase-table built on DEV). The translations of the OOVs were extracted from the word alignments of the base corpus, and out of 330 OOVs, 325 have gold translations.

The first two character-level models are just the unigram and bigram baseline models from Section 4.3. We then built further models by attempting to extract the *cognates* from the training set. The idea here is that the character-level models are built from "noisy" training data, containing many German-Viennese word-pairs which either represent lexical differences, or are the result of bad alignments. In order to extract the cognates we ran GIZA++ alignment on the combined TRAIN and DEV corpora, extracted all source-target token pairs that were aligned, converted the pairs to the BARSUBST representation (see section 5.1), and filtered using the log-normalised Levenshtein distance.

word-level:	`und für die tipps`
character-level (unigram):	`|| u n d || f ü r || d i e || t i p p s ||`
character-level (bigram):	`||u un nd d|| ||f fü ür r|| ||d di ie e|| ||t ti ip pp ps s||`

Figure 1: Conversion of a German sentence into forms suitable for training the character-level models

Model	Correct	Accuracy (%)
Pass-through	21	6.5
Unigram	154	47.4
Bigram	150	46.2
Unigram cognate	154	47.4
Bigram cognate	150	46.2
Unigram cognate (freq)	160	49.2
Bigram cognate (freq)	145	44.6

Table 2: Comparison of accuracy of character-level models on the OOVs in DEVTEST. The plain unigram/bigram models are trained on complete sentences, whereas the cognate models are trained on cognate pairs (unique or frequency weighted) extracted from these sentences.

With this list of cognate pairs, we trained both unigram and bigram models, firstly from a list of the unique cognate pairs and secondly from the same list with frequencies adjusted to match their corpus frequencies. These models were trained using the usual Moses pipeline, estimating phrase tables and language models from 90% of the cognate pairs and tuning on the other 10%.

The OOV accuracies (on DEVTEST) of all 6 character-level models, as well as a pass-through baseline are shown in Table 2. We can see that, in general, the cognate models offer small improvements on the models trained on the whole sentences, and the unigram models are slightly better than the bigram models.

Finally, we show a comparison of the word-level and character-level systems, with the backoff system (using the unigram cognate frequency adjusted model) in Table 3. The backoff systems are implemented by first examining the tuning and test data for OOVs, then translating these using the character-level model, and creating a second phrase-table with the character-level model. This second phrase table is used in Moses as a backoff table.

For both test sets, the character-level translation outperforms the word-level translation, but the backoff offers the best performance of all. The BLEU scores are relatively high compared to the typical values reported in the MT literature, reflecting the restricted vocabulary of the data set.

Model	DEVTEST	TEST
Word-level	63.28	60.04
Character-level (unigram)	65.00	63.17
Character-level (bigram)	64.98	63.43
Backoff to char-level	68.30	66.13

Table 3: BLEU scores for all translation systems

5 Comparable Corpora

Wikipedia is a multilingual free online encyclopedia with currently 285 language versions. Adafre and de Rijke (2006) investigated the potential of this resource to generate parallel corpora by applying different methods for identifying similar texts across multiple languages. We explore this resource as it contains a relatively large bilingual corpus of articles in (Standard) German (DE) and Bavarian dialects (BAR). There are 5135 parallel articles (status from July 2012), of which 219 are explicitly tagged as "Viennese dialect". It can be assumed that the parallel articles refer to the same content, but texts often differ substantially in style and detail. Articles in Bavarian are generally shorter, containing less information than the corresponding German ones, with an average ratio of about 1:6. The challenge of finding corresponding sentence pairs is met by a sentence alignment method that crucially exploits the phonetic similarity between the German standard and Bavarian dialects, specifically Viennese.

5.1 Sentence Extraction

Our sentence alignment algorithm is primarily based on string-edit distance measures. There exist several open-source alignment tools for extracting parallel sentences from bilingual corpora. However, none of them is applicable to our data because they either require a substantial amount of data to reliably estimate statistical models, i.e. at least 10k sentence pairs, such as the Microsoft Bilingual Aligner (Moore, 2002). But also the number of sentences to be aligned must be almost equal – with a ratio of 1:6 it was not possible to achieve any reliable results at all. Additionally, the sentences in the parallel texts are presupposed to occur in the same order, which does not apply to the Wikipedia articles under consideration. Similar requirements hold for the Hunalign tool (Varga et al., 2005). Finally, LEXACC (Stefanescu et al., 2012) is a parallel sentence extractor for comparable corpora based on Information Retrieval, but again, certain resources are required beforehand, such as a GIZA++ dictionary created from existing parallel documents. The main obstacle to using any of these algorithms is that the texts in the BAR Wikipedia obey widely differing and mostly ad-hoc orthographic conventions, which are not consistent for a given dialectal variety, even within a single article. In our situation, we had to develop an alignment method that relies only on the linguistic proximity between the two varieties.

Comparing strings of DE that occur in standard orthography with strings of BAR in varying non-standard orthography directly does not make sense, unless both forms are transformed into a phonetically based common form. Inspired by Soundex and the Kölner Phonetik algorithm (Postel, 1969), we developed an algorithm (henceforth BARSUBST) that takes into account some characteristics of the Bavarian dialect family (liquid vocalization: i.e., DE *'viel'* corresponds to VD: *'fü'*; vowels are retained as one class of characters; the character for 'dark a' <å> had to be included). This ensures that cognate words will have a very low string edit distance. Just to give an impression, we calculated the average values of Levenshtein string edit distance and the average ambiguity of particular word forms of AG and VD from the data of the word aligned base corpus. As ambiguity we counted the number of occurrences of a given word in a distinct word pair. The baseline value of 1.26/1.27 relates to the fact that for a given word there may be more than one valid translations. When the ambiguity is much higher this indicates that the distance measure is less reliable (words that should not relate turn out to be identical).

The average LD significantly drops down from 3.47 of the baseline (lowercase word forms) to approx. 1.0 for both, Kölner Phonetik and BARSUBST. The average ambiguity is almost equal for both BAR and DE - slightly below a value of 2 with BARSUBST; the Kölner Phonetik algorithm fares better with DE word forms, but worse with BAR word forms, which shows that it is justified to adapt the Kölner Phonetik algorithm to our purposes.

	LD	amb.DE	amb.VD
Baseline (lcase)	3.47	1.26	1.27
Soundex	1.35	4.53	5.69
Kölner Phonetik	1.00	1.87	2.25
BARSUBST	0.99	1.94	1.96

Table 4: Average distance and ambiguity values

Applying this algorithm to words of both DE and BAR, we defined a scoring function that evaluates possible word alignments against each other in order to find the optimal sentence pairs from related articles. The alignment algorithm works as follows: after creating a matrix of all sentence pairs, each potential alignment is evaluated by the scoring function that takes into account the sum of (positive and negative) scores resulting from a non-linear word alignment based on the transformed character sequences (best matches aligned first), the number of not-aligned words (negative scores) and a penalty for crossing alignments and extra short word sequences. We selected a set of approx. 50 sentences to manually test the effects of the different parameters of the scoring function. After fine-tuning the parameters, a threshold of above zero proved to be a good indicator for a correct alignment between two sentences. From this matrix, sentence pairs are extracted in the order of their scores (best scores aligned first) until a defined threshold is reached.

We used only articles that are explicitly tagged as 'Viennese' (approx. 200). From these we extracted and aligned 4414 sentences with 40.1k word tokens that correspond to 12.9k word types. Unlike the texts extracted from spontaneous speech recordings, the Wikipedia texts seem to contain many more word types, which is due to the fact that Wikipedia texts tend to contain a large number of named entities. Unfortunately, these are not very useful for SMT by themselves, but still the amount of parallel data can be significantly increased.

5.2 Orthography Normalization

One problem still to be solved in a satisfactory way is how to deal with non-standardized, inconsistent orthography in dialectal texts. The corpus of parallel sentences from Wikipedia articles can in principle provide ample training data for a character-level translation algorithm between non-standard orthography of BAR and our specifically designed, standardized orthography for VD. Given a 1-to-1 word alignment based on the Levenshtein distance of BARSUBST transformed word forms of sufficient quality, we can extract a list of BAR-DE word pairs, but the target, words in VD orthography, is missing.

To tackle this problem, we used the data from our speech-based corpus of aligned AG-VD word pairs. (We take Austrian German (AG) and German Standard (DE) to refer to the same variety). We filtered the list of word pairs gained from BAR-DE word alignment for only those DE-BAR pairs where we have an AG-VD word pair in our base corpus. That way, the AG/DE standard is used as an anchor to link non-standardized BAR orthography to our standard of DE orthography.

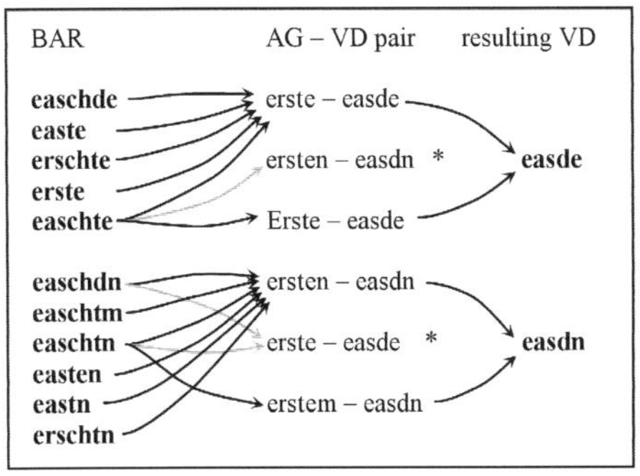

Figure 2: Correspondences between BAR orthographic forms, AG-VD pairs and VD forms.

As can be seen in Figure 2, the correspondences can be manifold. In order to decide which VD form is the correct one to be associated with certain BAR variants, we apply a weighted Levenshtein distance measure, where the weights are chosen in such a way that plausible and frequent substitutions are assigned less costs than others. When more data is available, these weights can be re-estimated on a statistical basis, for a start we just stipulated them based on the linguistic knowledge about the two varieties. The matches are not symmetrical under this approach, for example BAR <m> matching with VD <n> (which often occurs when dative endings in BAR are written according to the standard of DE, while they are pronounced and written as /n/ in VD) is assigned a cost of 0.6, while the reverse match is not defined and receives the default cost value of 1.)

Having gathered some initial training data this way, we experimented to train a character level translation using again Sequitur G2P. Of all the pairs, we spared 25% for testing and used the rest for training, which proved to be very little – approx. 1500 instances of BAR-VD pairs. To increase this number in a sensible way, we created two more sets by adding the set of AG-VD pairs from the base corpus and adding the set of VD-VD pairs, simulating a situation where the BAR input is already in the correct orthography. The results are not fully compelling (50 % correct spellings in the optimal case). This may be due to the rather small amount of training data, but also to the high degree of variance in the input data. To enhance the quality of orthography normalization we foresee a combination of modelling character-level BAR-VD correspondences with the character-level translation models of AG to VD that hopefully will make it possible to achieve a automatically normalized parallel corpus from the Wikipedia data that conforms to the same standards as the base corpus.

6 Discussion and Outlook

Starting from a base corpus of parallel AG and VD sentences generated by manual transcription of spoken text and translation into the two varieties, we applied various methods to iteratively enhance the word alignment and the generation of lexical resources in the target variety. Using this corpus for SMT provided good preliminary results given that we employed a backoff strategy for OOV words building on character level models. To enlarge the corpus with automatic methods, we extracted sentence pairs from corresponding articles from the Bavarian and the German Wikipedia, where the identification of corresponding sentences was based on the similarity of the two varieties. Still, the normalization of Bavarian/Viennese dialectal spelling to our orthography is work in progress. However, methods for normalization of spelling are crucial for the acquisition of monolingual data from texts in dialects, generally. Another line will be the bootstrapping of parallel data by generating automatic translations of sentences that are selected by an active learning algorithm, in order to gain maximal information for the system.

References

Sadaf Abdul-Rauf and Holger Schwenk. 2011. Parallel sentence generation from comparable corpora for improved SMT. *Machine Transl.*, 25(4):341–375.

Sisay Fissaha Adafre and Maarten de Rijke. 2006. Finding similar sentences across multiple languages in wikipedia. In *Proceedings of the 11th Conference of the European Association for Computational Linguistics (EACL)*, pages 62–69.

Maximilian Bisani and Hermann Ney. 2008. Joint-sequence models for grapheme-to-phoneme conversion. *Speech Communication*, 50(5):434–451.

Peter F. Brown, Vincent J. Della Pietra, Stephen A. Della Pietra, and Robert L. Mercer. 1993. The mathematics of statistical machine translation: parameter estimation. *Comp. Ling.*, 19(2):263–311.

Maria Hornung. 1998. *Wörterbuch der Wiener Mundart*. ÖBV, Pädagogischer Verlag.

Philipp Koehn and Hieu Hoang. 2007. Factored translation models. In *Proceedings of the 2007 Joint Conference on Empirical Methods in Natural Language Processing and Computational Natural Language Learning (EMNLP-CoNLL)*, pages 868–876, Prague, Czech Republic, June.

Philipp Koehn, Hieu Hoang, Alexandra Birch, Chris Callison-Burch, Marcello Federico, Nicola Bertoldi, Brooke Cowan, Wade Shen, Christine Moran, Richard Zens, Chris Dyer, Ondrej Bojar, Alexandra Constantin, and Evan Herbst. 2007. Moses: open source toolkit for statistical machine translation. In *Proceedings of the 45th Annual Meeting of the Association for Computational Linguistics (ACL), demonstration session*, pages 177–180, Prague, Czech Republic.

William Labov. 2001. *Principles of linguistic change (ii): social factors*. Blackwell, Massachusetts.

Robert C. Moore. 2002. Fast and accurate sentence alignment of bilingual corpora. In *Proceedings of the 5th Conference of the Association for Machine Translation in the Americas (AMTA)*, pages 135–144, Tiburon, CA.

Dragos Stefan Munteanu and Daniel Marcu. 2005. Improving machine translation performance by exploiting non-parallel corpora. *Computational Linguistics*, 31(4):477–504.

Preslav Nakov and Jörg Tiedemann. 2012. Combining word-level and character-level models for machine translation between closely-related languages. In *Proceedings of the 50th Annual Meeting of the Association for Computational Linguistics*, pages 301–305, Jeju, Korea.

Franz Josef Och and Hermann Ney. 2000. Improved Statistical Alignment Models. In *Proceedings of the 38th Annual Meeting of the Association for Computational Linguistics (ACL00)*, pages 440–447, Hongkong, China.

Hans Joachim Postel. 1969. Die Kölner Phonetik. Ein Verfahren zur Identifizierung von Personennamen auf der Grundlage der Gestaltanalyse. *IBM-Nachrichten*, 19:925–931.

Hassan Sawaf. 2010. Arabic dialect handling in hybrid machine translation. In *Proceedings of the 9th Conference of the Association for Machine Translation in the Americas (AMTA)*, Denver, Colorado.

Hans Schikola. 1954. *Schriftdeutsch und Wienerisch*. Österr. Bundesverlag für Unterricht, Wissenschaft und Kunst.

Jason R. Smith, Chris Quirk, and Kristina Toutanova. 2010. Extracting parallel sentences from comparable corpora using document level alignment. In *Proceedings of Human Language Technologies: The 2010 Annual Conference of the North American Chapter*, pages 403–411, Los Angeles, California.

Dan Stefanescu, Radu Ion, and Sabine Hunsicker. 2012. Hybrid parallel sentence mining from comparable corpora. In *Proceedings of the 16th Annual Conference of the European Association for Machine Translation (EMAT)*, pages 137–144, Trento, Italy.

Jörg Tiedemann. 2009. Character-based {PSMT} for closely related languages. In Lluís Marqués and Harold Somers, editors, *Proceedings of 13th Annual Conference of the European Association for Machine Translation (EAMT'09)*, pages 12–19, Barcelona, Spain.

Christoph Tillmann and Jian-Ming Xu. 2009. A simple sentence-level extraction algorithm for comparable data. In *Proceedings of Human Language Technologies: The 2009 Annual Conference of the North American Chapter of the Association for Computational Linguistics*, pages 93–96, Boulder, Colorado.

Dániel Varga, Péter Halácsy, András Kornai, Viktor Nagy, Lászlo Németh, and Viktor Trón. 2005. Parallel corpora for medium density languages. In *Proceedings of the RANLP*, pages 590–596.

David Vilar, Jan-Thorsten Peter, and Hermann Ney. 2007. Can we translate letters? In *Proceedings of the Second Workshop on Statistical Machine Translation*, pages 33–39, Prague, Czech Republic. Association for Computational Linguistics.

Rabih Zbib, Erika Malchiodi, Jacob Devlin, David Stallard, Spyros Matsoukas, Richard Schwartz, John Makhoul, Omar F. Zaidan, and Chris Callison-Burch. 2012. Machine translation of Arabic dialects. In *Proceedings of the 2012 Conference of the North American Chapter of the Association for Computational Linguistics: Human Language Technologies (NAACL HLT)*, pages 49–59, Montreal, Canada.

Adaptation of a Rule-Based Translator to Río de la Plata Spanish

Ernesto López
Instituto de Computación
Universidad de la República
Uruguay
ernesto.nicolas.lopez@gmail.com

Luis Chiruzzo
Instituto de Computación
Universidad de la República
Uruguay
luischir@fing.edu.uy

Dina Wonsever
Instituto de Computación
Universidad de la República
Uruguay
wonsever@fing.edu.uy

Abstract

Pronominal and verbal voseo is a well-established variant in spoken language, and also very common in some written contexts - web sites, literary works, screenplays or subtitles - in Rio de la Plata Spanish. An implementation of Río de la Plata Spanish (including voseo) was made in the open source collaborative system Apertium, whose design is suited for the development of new translation pairs. This work includes: development of a translation pair for Río de la Plata Spanish-English (back and forth), based on the Spanish-English pairs previously included in Apertium; creation of a bilingual corpus based on subtitles of movies; evaluation on this corpus of the developed Apertium variant by comparing it to the original Apertium version and to a statistical translator in the state of the art.

1 Introduction

In this multilingual world, easily accessible through Internet, machine translation is becoming increasingly important. While the problem as a whole remains yet to be solved, there are several systems which provide an interesting service, by automatically producing a translated version of a text. In these days Google (Google, 2013) provides translation services - at least from and into English - for 51 different languages. While, in general, translations provided by Google are not completely accurate, users will have a reasonable comprehension of the content of the source text. A language like Spanish, that is spoken by about 420 million people (Instituto Cervantes, 2012) and is the official language in 21 countries, covering a vast geographical region, has different regional variations, some of which are firmly well-established. Appropriate coverage and fluid texts, adjusted to the situation and the language registry of an utterance, are not possible unless machine translation systems contemplate the consolidated and accepted variants used.

Pronominal and verbal *voseo* is a well-established variant in spoken language, and also very common in some written contexts - web sites, literary works, screenplays or subtitles - in Rio de la Plata Spanish.[1] To include this variant in a statistical machine translation system requires the availability of a large corpus for the language pair involved. An implementation of Río de la Plata Spanish (including *voseo*) was made in the open source collaborative system Apertium (Forcada et al., 2011), whose design is suited for the development of new translation pairs.

This work includes: development of a translation pair Río de la Plata Spanish-English (back and forth), based on the Spanish-English pairs previously included in Apertium; creation of a bilingual corpus based on subtitles of movies; evaluation on this corpus of the developed Apertium variant by comparing it to the original Apertium version and to a statistical translator in the state of the art. There is also an improvement of the translation system, through the addition of a repertoire of proper nouns of Uruguayan geographical regions.

The following section briefly introduces machine translation systems and their current performance. Section 3 describes the use of *voseo* in Río de la Plata while sections 4 and 5 describe the system development, the creation of the corpus, the evaluation and its results. Conclusions are in section 6. The developed translation pairs and the evaluation corpus are both available.

[1] This region includes an important part of Argentina and almost the entire Uruguayan territory.

2 Background

Machine translation (MT) is a development area within Natural Language Processing, which relates to the use of automatic tools to translate texts from one natural language into another. The different approaches used to solve this problem are separated into two main groups: Rule-based Machine Translation (RBMT) and Statistical Machine Translation (SMT).

2.1 Statistical Machine Translation

The current state of the art in MT is provided by Statistical Machine Translation systems. The initial interest into these approaches was drawn by the work of Brown et al. (1993), which recommends developing a *translation model* between language pairs and a *language model* for the target language. The system finds the best sentence in the target language, maximizing both accuracy (translation model) and fluency (language model).

Today the best performances are provided by phrase-based systems (PBMT) (Koehn et al., 2003). These systems consider the alignment of complete phrases in their translation model, and incorporate a *phrase reordering model*.

SMT systems strongly depend on the existence of a large volume of linguistic resources. Particularly, they depend on a target language corpus and a parallel corpus in source and target languages. This information is not available in an important number of language pairs.

2.2 Rule-Based Machine Translation

The second group of MT methods are the Rule-Based Machine Translation methods. These methods apply manually crafted rules to translate the source language text into the target language.

Usually, translations produced by these methods are more mechanic than and not as fluent as those produced by SMT. However, users who have a fairly good command of both languages do not require large parallel corpora to elaborate translation rules (Forcada et al., 2011).

2.3 Hybrid Machine Translation

In recent years, new approaches have attempted to combine the best qualities of the two traditional groups of translation systems (Thurmair, 2009). Statistical Post-Edition (SPE) edits manually the output of a RBMT system to produce a higher-quality translation. Then, a corpus is created using the RBMT output and the edited translation, and a SMT is trained with this corpus [Simard 2007].

By using a parallel corpus, Molchanov (2012) extracts a bilingual dictionary and complements it with SPE between the RBMT output and the parallel corpus destiny. Dugast et al. (2008) trains a SMT with the correspondence of the source text and the RBMT translation, instead of using a parallel corpus or a manually corrected output.

There is a different hybrid approach which uses phrases translated by the Apertium system (RBMT) to enrich the translation model tables of the Moses system (SMT) (Sanchez-Cartagena et al., 2011).

2.4 Apertium

Apertium is a RBMT system developed by the *Transducens group* from the *Universitat d'Alacant*. Originally, it was a translation system for related-language pairs (particularly for languages spoken in Spain) (Corbi-Bellot et al., 2005), but later on modules were added to translate more distant language pairs, such as English and Spanish (Forcada et al., 2011).

It is an open-source machine translation platform and it includes a set of tools to develop new language pairs. For this reason, an important number of collaborators have contributed with new linguistic resources and there are currently 36 pairs (Apertium, 2013) of languages officially accepted to be translated by Apertium.

Apertium has proved to be very useful to develop translation systems between related languages (Wiechetek et al., 2010) and languages with few linguistic resources (Martinez et al., 2012). In other development areas Apertium has been integrated to other finite-state tools such as the Helsinki Finite-State Toolkit (Washington et al., 2012).

As mentioned above, besides being used as a standalone RBMT system, there have been some experiments regarding the use of Apertium jointly with statistical systems (Sanchez-Cartagena et al., 2011).

3 Río de la Plata Spanish

There are variants in all languages spoken in the world. These are differences in vocabulary, verb conjugation, pronunciation, and in some cases, even syntactic differences.

Language variants are caused by historical, cultural and geographical factors. There are many sociological studies which try to explain the reason for these variants. For example, Chilean Spanish, which has a fairly unusual pronunciation, is a combination of the language spoken by Mapuche natives and the Quechua language from the south. This Spanish variant is found even in Argentinean provinces bordering with Chile. It has a lot in common with Rio de la Plata Spanish. Even in Uruguay, with a small population – just over 3 million people – there are multiple variants of Spanish. In Uruguayan cities separated by street borders from Brazil, there is a particular combination of Spanish and Portuguese. There is another example in southern Brazil, where Portuguese language uses the personal pronoun 'tú' (you singular).

The Spanish spoken in Río de la Plata is no exception, with many differences with Spanish from Spain. This variant occurs mainly in coast cities along Río de la Plata and Río Uruguay, upstream to the mouth of Río Negro. But it is also found in Uruguayan remote inland, albeit with variants, with a stronger Portuguese influence. Likewise, fusion of Spanish variants is seen in northern Argentina provinces and in southern Paraguay (Elizaincín, 2009).

There are various differences between Río de la Plata Spanish and the other Spanish variants. Some of these differences are only phonetic, such as *yeísmo* [2], and others are related to verb conjugation and pronoun uses, such as *voseo*. *Voseo* - albeit not exclusively from Río de la Plata - is one of the most distinctive particularities of this Spanish variant, and it itself has some variants. In the definition of RAE[3] *voseo* is the use of the pronominal *vos* (You, singular) to address the interlocutor (RAE, 2011). There are two separate types of *voseo*:

The **reverential *voseo***, is the ceremonial usage of *vos* pronoun to address the second person, both plural and singular, and it is rarely used today. It is found in old Spanish texts, ceremonial writings or those which recreate Spanish language from the past.

The subject of this work is the **South American dialectal *voseo***. It is the Spanish use of the plural second-person pronominal and (modified) verbal forms, to address a single interlocutor. It is common in different variants of Spanish in Latin America, and, unlike reverential *voseo*, it implies closeness and informality since it is not usually seen - at least in its pronominal form - in very formal situations, where *ustedeo* is commonly used (Kapovic, 2007). The conjugation pattern in this variant is also different to peninsular Spanish.

Pronominal *voseo*

Pronominal *voseo* is the use of *vos* as singular second-person pronoun, instead of *tú* or *ti*. *Vos* is used as:

- Subject: *Puede que **vos** tengás razón* (**You** might be right)
- Vocative: *¿Por qué la tenés contra Alvaro Arzú, **vos**?* (**You**, what is it that you have against Alvaro Arzú?)
- Preposition term: *Cada vez que sale con **vos**, se enferma* (Every time he goes out with **you**, he feels unwell)
- Comparison term: *Es por lo menos tan actor como **vos*** (He is so good an actor as **you**)

According to RAE, for pronouns used with pronominal verbs and in objects with no preposition (atonic pronoun), and for possessive pronouns, it is combined with *tuteo* form, e.g.: *Vos **te** lavaste las manos* (You washed your hands), *No cerrés **tus** ojos* (Don't close your eyes).

Verbal *voseo*

Verbal *voseo* is more complex than pronominal *voseo*. RAE defines "verbal *voseo* is the use of the original verb suffixes of the plural second-person, more or less modified, in the conjugating forms of the singular second-person: *tú vivís, vos comés, vos comís* (you live, you eat, you eat)*"*. Verbs vary differently in their form and tenses in each region. Complexity of verbal *voseo* lies on the fact that its use varies considerably in each region, some of which do not accept it as correct language. The subject of this work is the Río de la Plata variant. In fact, *voseo* is acknowledged as correct language only in Argentina, Uruguay and Paraguay (Kapovic, 2007). The Argentine Academy of Letters did not accept *voseo* as correct language – and only in some of its modalities - until 1982.

Voseo, as mentioned above, implies closeness and informality, and this is strongly related with its origin. Originally, it was rejected by purists and considered vulgar and demeaning by grammarians of the time. The use of *vos* was firmly rejected, particularly by the upper-class society.

---

[2] ***Yeísmo*** consists of a phonological variant, where consonants /ĭ/ and /y/ are merged into a single sound /y/. It is a phonological process which merges two phonemes originally different (González, 2011).

[3] Royal Spanish Academy

Present tense verbal voseo

It may be found in indicative present tense forms combined with the plural diphthongs (*habláis (*You talk*)*); in some cases the **s** at the end of the verb is silent, particularly in Andean regions. In Río de la Plata, diphthongs consist of a single open vowel (*sabés (*You know*)*), although there are documents in which the vowel is closed (*sabís (*You know*)*). For first conjugation verbs, where infinitive forms end in *-ar*, verbs do not end in *–ís* with *vos* in this present tense form (RAE, 2011).

In present subjunctive structures *voseo* is seen in plural diphthongs as well (*habléis (...*you to talk), in some regions the *s* at the end of the verb is silent. In Río de la Plata, diphthongs consist of a single open vowel (*subás (...*you to climb*)*), although there are documents in which the vowel is closed (*hablís (...*you to talk*)*). Here, the *–ís* suffix only appears in first conjugation verbs.

Verbal voseo in imperative tenses

Voseo in imperative tenses is the variation of the plural second-person with omission of the *d* at the end of the verb. For example: *tomá (tomad (*take*)), poné (poned (*put*))*. These forms do not follow irregularities of the singular second-person characteristic of *tuteo*, therefore, *di (tell), sal (leave), ven (come), ten* (take) become *decí, salí, vení, tené* in verbal *voseo*.

These verb forms have accent marks since they are words stressed on the last syllable with a vowel at the end. When there is a pronoun attached to the verb, as a suffix, these forms follow general accentuation rules. For example: "*Compenetrate en Beethoven, imaginátelo. Imaginate su melena"* (RAE, 2011). ("Think about Beethoven, picture him. Picture his long hair" (RAE, 2011).

Pronominal and verbal *voseo* may be combined with *tuteo*. These are the modalities of *voseo*:

- Verbal and pronominal use of *vos*: Very frequently used in Río de la Plata. The subject, *vos*, is combined with verbal *voseo* forms, e.g.: "*Vos no podés entregarles los papeles antes de setenta y dos horas" (*You cannot give him the documents for the next three days*)*
- Exclusively verbal *voseo*: The subject of the verbal forms in this case is exclusively *tú*. It is commonly used in Uruguay, particularly in fairly informal situations.
- Exclusively pronominal *voseo*: *Vos* is the subject of singular second-person verbs, e.g.: "*Vos tienes la culpa para hacerte tratar mal*" (You are the one to blame for his abusive behaviour). This is rare in Río de la Plata.

4 Río de la Plata Apertium

Apertium decomposes the translation process into modules, executed in sequence. Figure 1 describes the pipeline of Apertium modules. It may be divided into the following steps:

- De-formatter: Separates the text in the input file from the format information.
- Morphological analyzer: In this module the text is segmented into lexical units. The units are supplied with morphological information. This step requires finite-state transducers (FST) technology.

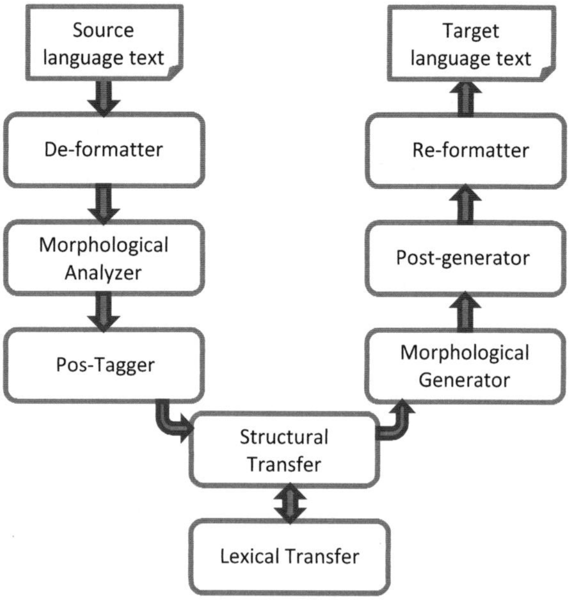

Figure 1 - Apertium modules

- POS-Tagger: The part-of-speech tagger chooses one of these analyses for the lexical unit.
- Lexical transfer: Establishes correspondence of the lexical units in the target language with the lexical units from the source text.
- Structural transfer: There is shallow parsing or chunking of text and a set of rules are applied, established specifically for each language pair, to transform the source language structure into the structure of the target language. Therefore, Apertium is classified as a shallow transfer system. (Forcada et al., 2010)
- Morphological generator: The morphological generator inflects target-language lexical units to produce the surface forms.

- Post-generator: Applies target-language orthographic rules.
- Re-formatter: Restores format information encapsulated by the de-formatter, to produce a translated file format similar to the source file format.

Voseo is a discourse phenomenon, occurring basically at morphological level. In Apertium, this process is carried out by the morphological analyzer. There is a transducer generated from an XML file, including the necessary rules (Forcada et al., 2011). The input of the module is a set of lexical units which are separately processed, inflections are analysed, and based on inflections, the attributes of the unit, such as lexical category, number or gender (for verbs) are tagged. The XML file information consists simply of rules which assign a set of attributes to a particular morphology.

In the particular case of verbs and verb tenses, verbs with similar morphological inflection – even if their lemma is different – belong to the same group. For example, in Spanish the verbs *cantar* (to sing) and *abandonar* (to abandon) have similar morphological inflection. Therefore, inflection paradigms are independent from lemmas.

	Cantaría	**Abandonaría**
Lemma	Cant	Abandon
Inflection	aría	aría
Attributes	Verb, Cond., Indic., Sing., First Person	Verb, Cond., Indic., Sing., First Person

Table 1 - Verbal paradigms in Apertium

It is clear that there are multiple analyses for each lexical unit. The selection of the corresponding analysis occurs in the next module. A new verb may be added by simply identifying its lemma and selecting an inflection paradigm. Therefore, since verbal *voseo* modifies verb inflections, this variation may be included by simply adding the new inflections to the paradigms already defined for traditional Spanish. So all the verbal paradigms defined in the Apertium dictionary were extracted, and the inflections studied and their corresponding attributes for imperative tenses and indicative present tenses were added. There were 170 inflection paradigms modified.

For pronominal *voseo*, the lexical unit *vos* was added to the dictionary. It was assigned with the attribute of tonic pronoun.

To improve the identification of named entities, 120 locations of Uruguay were added to the Apertium dictionary. They were extracted from the Geonames database (Geonames, 2011).

5 Evaluation and metrics

It is extremely complex to evaluate a translation system, mainly because there is usually more than one correct translation. Translations may vary in the word order, and even use different words. Yet translations will have many things in common and this is what metrics tries to measure to evaluate machine translation systems (Papineni et al., 2002).

A reference translation is always used to evaluate the MT system and sentences are the basic evaluation units every time. One of the most acknowledged metrics is BLEU, which weighs adequacy and fluency of sentences. This requires considering not only the number of lexical units in common between the translation to be evaluated and the reference translation, but also the length of common n-grams. BLEU also penalizes translation lengths which do not match the reference translation (Papineni et al., 2002).

NIST metrics - also used to evaluate translation systems - was also taken into account in this work. NIST is based on BLEU. The only difference is that NIST gives a higher score to less common n-grams, which actually provide more information to the content of the sentence.

5.1 Evaluation corpus

The corpus to evaluate the adaptation of Apertium should have the following particularities: It should be a bilingual Spanish – English corpus, for Río de la Plata Spanish, contemplating that *voseo* is more frequent in dialogues and conversations.

There are some texts that contain dialogues and conversations, which naturally have translations: movie subtitles. There are many movies subtitled in several languages. These subtitles may be read as transcriptions of the same text, in different languages, so subtitles are bilingual texts. Although it fails to be a perfectly aligned corpus, a very valuable asset of subtitles is the time window where they must be shown on screen. This provides more information, which is very useful to align two subtitles from the same movie.

It is very simple to find subtitles in the web. However, the only subtitles of interest for this work were those which included texts in Río de la Plata Spanish. IMDb highest-ranked movies from Argentina and Uruguay were used based on the premise that it is more likely to find the corresponding subtitles in both languages. Whenever possible, the original transcription extracted from the movies' official version was used. Otherwise, the subtitles used were those created by Internet users, based on the same highest-ranked premise. A corpus with about 100000 words was elaborated by using subtitles from 26 movies (Table 2).

Name	Year
The Pope's Toilet	2007
Son of the Bride	2001
Valentín	2002
Waiting for the Hearse	1985
Merry Christmas	2000
Official Story	1985
Night of the pencils	1986
The Die is Cast	2005
Rain	2008
Nine Queens	2000
Chinese Take-Away	2011
Avellaneda's moon	2004
A Matter of Principles	2009
Made Up Memories	2008
Martin (Hache)	1997
Camila	1984
Tierra del Fuego	2000
Seawards Journey	2003
Whisky	2004
25 Watts	2001
A place in the world	1992
Burnt Money	2000
Autumn sun	1996
Chronicle of an Escape	2006
Anita	2009
On Probation	2005

Table 2 - Movies used for the evaluation corpus

Sentences were aligned in all subtitles based on (Tyers and Pienaar, 2008; Tiedemann, 2007; Gale and Church, 1991; Brown et al., 1991). Sentences from subtitle pairs were aligned with relative precision, using the start/end time of the lines in the screen. In general, the parallelization algorithm groups together those sentences that appear in the same time frame in the subtitle pair. Then sentences are aligned based on their length, given similar sentence lengths in both languages. Accuracy was about 80% for random samples.

5.2 Evaluation and results

NIST and BLEU metrics were used. Adaptations made were compared with Apertium in its traditional version and with Google translator. Evaluation scripts (NIST, 2011) used were those developed in the 2008 edition of the NIST (National Institute of Standards and Technology) Open Machine Translation Evaluation.

In Spanish to English translations, all results provided by Apertium adapted to Río de la Plata Spanish were more correct translations than those obtained with Apertium's traditional version. As expected, Google translator provides significantly better results. Table 3 shows the average results for these metrics, in the Spanish into English direction.

	BLEU	NIST
Traditional Apertium	0.118183333	3.414683333
Río de la Plata Apertium	0.1246	3.553916667
Google Translator	0.226116667	4.810316667

Table 3 - Spanish into English translation results

The amount of *voseo* occurrences contained in the source text is difficult to establish, yet there is a 5.4% increase in the performance of Apertium in relation to the traditional version of the system. The modified system identifies the *voseo* verbs and its contractions, as well as all the uses of the *vos* pronoun.

In terms of recognition, the analysis of the morphological analyser output showed 13% and 14% improvement in the recognition of verbs and pronouns, respectively. Recognition improvement of named entities was 4.4%, reflecting that 44% more locations were identified.

While Google Translator provides better results, this is mainly due to the fact that generally translations are structurally and lexically more accurate. Many lexical units are not included in Apertium's dictionaries, which could explain its recognition problems, as shown in Table 4. In terms of *voseo*, Google Translator does not handle the *vos* pronoun properly: Google translator translates '*Vos pensás en él*' as '**Vos you think on it*'.

Translation for:	Vos te lo merecés
Apertium	* Vos You it * merecés
R.P. Apertium	You deserve it

Table 4 - Translation before and after adaptation

In English to Spanish translations (Table 5), a fact to consider is that the Río de la Plata Apertium translator may operate in two modes to produce Spanish text: in the traditional mode (exclusively use of *tú*) or in the mode with exclusive use of *vos*. The traditional mode and the system without modifications provide identical results. Therefore, the work studied the operation of the system in the modality with exclusive use of *vos*.

	BLEU	NIST
Traditional Apertium	0.112733333	3.35635
Río de la Plata Apertium	0.111433333	3.374283333
Google Translator	0.21005	4.597533333

Table 5 - English into Spanish translation results

6 Conclusions

Apertium machine translations were improved by generating Río de la Plata Spanish – English pairs in the system. This is a free tool, and will be useful to translate colloquial language texts, such as web sites, blogs, literary works, screenplays or subtitles.

A Río de la Plata Spanish – English bilingual corpus was compilated from movie subtitles. This corpus was aligned and used for evaluation. There was clear improvement in relation to the previous version of Apertium. Apertium was compared with Google Translator at all times and in this context, Google Translator clearly surpasses Apertium. However, while Google Translator's performance is always better, there were some examples in which it failed to deal with the *voseo* particularity.

Translation was also improved by the addition of geographical entity names from the Geonames repository, filtered by their importance.

Overall, in translations from Río de la Plata Spanish into English, there is clear improvement, while not in the opposite direction, since *voseo* and traditional variants co-exist. So a more refined mechanism is required, to capture the speech registry in each statement and to select the corresponding mode. In future works, communicative situations and participants should be contemplated, as well as the symmetric and asymmetric interpersonal relations involved.

References

Apertium. 2013. Wiki – Apertium, Main Page. http://wiki.apertium.org/wiki/Main_Page (7th July, 2013)

Peter F. Brown, Jennifer Lai and Robert Mercer. 1991. *Aligning sentences in parallel corpora.* ACL.

Peter F. Brown, Stephen A. Della Pietra, Vincent J. Della Pietra and Robert L. Mercer. 1993. *The Mathematics of Statistical Machine Translation.* IBM T.J. Watson Research Center. Computational Linguistics - Special issue on using large corpora: II archive Volume 19 Issue 2, June 1993. Pages 263-311. MIT Press Cambridge, MA, USA.

Antonio M. Corbí-Bellot, Mikel L. Forcada, Sergio Ortiz-Rojas, Juan Antonio Pérez Ortiz, Gema Ramírez-Sánchez, Felipe Sánchez-Martínez, Iñaki Alegria, Aingeru Mayor and Kepa Sarasola. 2005. *An Open-Source Shallow-Transfer Machine Translation Engine for the Romance Languages of Spain.* Proceedings of the European Assocītation for Machine Translation, 10th Annual Conference (Budapest, Hungary, 30-31.05.2005), p. 79-86.

Loïc Dugast, Jean Senellart and Philipp Koehn. 2008. *Can we relearn an RBMT system?* Proceedings of the Third Workshop on Statistical Machine Translation, pages 175–178, Columbus, Ohio, USA, June 2008.

Adolfo Elizaincín. 2009. *Geolingüística, sustrato y contacto lingüístico: español, portugués e italiano en uruguay.* ROSAE – Congresso em Homenagem a Rosa Virgínia Mattos e Silva.

Mikel L. Forcada, Boyan Ivanov Bonev, Sergio Ortiz Rojas, Juan Antonio Perez Ortiz, Gema Ramirez Sanchez, Felipe Sanchez Martinez, Carme Armentano-Oller, Marco A. Montava and Francis M. Tyers. 2010. *Documentation of the Open-Source Shallow-Transfer Machine Translation Platform Apertium.*

Mikel L. Forcada, Mireia Ginestí-Rosell, Jacob Nordfalk, Jim O'Regan, Sergio Ortiz-Rojas, Juan Antonio Pérez-Ortiz, Felipe Sánchez-Martínez, Gema Ramírez-Sánchez and Francis M. Tyers. 2011. *Apertium: a free/open-source platform for rule-based machine translation.* Machine Translation: Volume 25, Issue 2 (2011), p. 127-144.

William A. Gale and Kenneth W. Church. 1991. *A program for aligning sentences in bilingual corpora.* ACL '91 Proceedings of the 29th annual meeting on Association for Computational Linguistics.

Geonames Web Site. *About Geonames.* http://www.geonames.org/about.html (23rd September, 2011).

Google Translate. 2013. http://translate.google.com/ (23rd July, 2013)

Rosario González Galicia. 2011. *Mi querida elle.* http://www.babab.com/no09/elle.htm (2nd August, 2011)

Instituto Cervantes. 2012. *Primer estudio conjunto del Instituto Cervantes y el British Council sobre el peso internacional del español y del inglés.* Instituto Cervantes. 21st June, 2012. http://www.cervantes.es/sobre_instituto_cervantes/prensa/2012/noticias/nota-londres-palabra-por-palabra.htm

Marko Kapovic. 2007. *Fórmulas de tratamiento en dialectos de español, fenómenos de voseo y ustedeo.* HIERONYMUS I, 2007.

Philipp Koehn, Franz Josef Och and Daniel Marcu. 2003. *Statistical Phrase-Based Translation.* HLT/NAACL 2003.

Juan Pablo Martínez Cortes, Jim O'Regan and Francis M. Tyers. 2012. *Free/Open Source Shallow-Transfer Based Machine Translation for Spanish and Aragonese.* LREC 2012.

Alexander Molchanov. 2012. *PROMT DeepHybrid system for WMT12 shared translation task.* Proceedings of the 7th Workshop on Statistical Machine Translation, pages 345–348, Montreal, Canada, June 7-8, 2012.

NIST. 2008. Mt08 scoring scripts. http://www.itl.nist.gov/iad/mig//tests/mt/2008/scoring.html, (23rd September, 2011)

Kishore Papineni, Salim Roukos, Todd Ward, and Wei-Jing Zhu. 2002. *Bleu: A method for automatic evaluation of machine translation.* 40th Annual Meeting of the Association for Computational Linguistics (ACL), Philadelphia, July 2002, pp. 311-318.

Real Academia Española. 2011. *Diccionario panhispánico de dudas, 1era edición 2da tirada.* http://buscon.rae.es/dpdI/SrvltGUIBusDPD?lema=voseo, (5th October, 2011)

Víctor M. Sanchez-Cartagena, Felipe Sánchez-Martínez and Juan Antonio Perez-Ortiz. 2011. *Integrating shallow-transfer rules into phrase-based statistical machine translation.* Proceedings of the 13th Machine Translation Summit : September 19-23, 2011, Xiamen, China, pp. 562-569

Michel Simard, Cyril Goutte and Pierre Isabelle. 2007. *Statistical Phrase-based Post-editing.* Proceedings of NAACL.

Jörg Tiedemann. 2007. *Improved sentence alignment for movie subtitles.* In Proceedings of RANLP 2007, Borovets, Bulgaria, pages 582–588, 2007.

Gregor Thurmair. 2009. *Comparing different architectures of hybrid MachineTranslation systems.* MT Summit XII: proceedings of the twelfth Machine Translation Summit, August 26-30, 2009, Ottawa, Ontario, Canada; pp.340-347.

Francis M. Tyers and Jacques A. Pienaar. 2008. *Extracting bilingual word pairs from wikipedia.* Proceedings of the SALTMIL Workshop at Language Resources and Evaluation Conference., LREC08:19–22.

Jonathan North Washington, Mirlan Ipasov and Francis M. Tyers. 2012. *A finite-state morphological transducer for Kyrgyz.* LREC 2012.

Linda Wiechetek, Francis M. Tyers and Thomas Omma. 2010. *Shooting at flies in the dark: Rule-based lexical selection for a minority language pair.* Proceeding IceTAL'10 Proceedings of the 7th international conference on Advances in natural language processing. Pages 418-429.

Text segmentation for Language Identification in Greek Forums

Pavlina Fragkou
Technological Educational Institution of Athens (TEI-A),
Dept. of Informatics Systems,
Ag. Spyridonos, 12210, Egaleo, Athens, Greece.
pfragkou@teiath.gr

Abstract

In this paper, we examine the benefit of applying text segmentation methods to perform language identification in forums. The focus here is on forums containing a mixture of information written in Greek, English as well as Greeklish. Greeklish can be defined as the use of Latin alphabet for rendering Greek words with Latin characters. For the evaluation, a corpus was manually created by collecting web pages from Greek university forums and most specifically, pages containing information that combines Greek with English technical terminology and Greeklish. The evaluation using two well known text segmentation algorithms leads to the conclusion that despite the difficulty of the problem examined, text segmentation seems to be a promising solution.

1 Introduction

Language identification can be defined as the process of determining which natural language given content is in. Traditionally, identification of written language - as practiced for instance in library science - has relied on manually identifying frequent words and letters known to be characteristic of particular languages. More recently, computational approaches have been applied to the problem, by viewing language identification as a special case of text categorization, a Natural Language Processing approach that relies on a statistical method.

Greeklish, which comes from the combination of the words Greek and English, stands for the Greek language written using the Latin alphabet. The term Greeklish mainly refers to informal, adhoc practices of writing Greek text in environments where the use of the Greek alphabet is technically impossible or cumbersome, especially in electronic media. Greeklish was commonly used on the Internet when Greek people communicate by forum, e-mail, instant messaging and occasionally on SMS, mainly because older operating systems didn't have the ability to write in Greek, or in a Unicode form like UTF-8. Nowadays, most Greek language content appears in native Greek alphabet.

This paper is organized as follows: Section 2 provides information regarding related work, Section 3 provides a description of the method followed and the algorithms used, Section 4 provides evaluation metrics and obtained results, while Section 5 provides concluding remarks and future work.

2 Related Work

Language identification cannot be considered as a novel scientific area. Language identification of text has become increasingly important as large quantities of text are processed or filtered automatically for tasks such as information retrieval or machine translation. The problem has been researched long both in the text and in the speech domain.

Several works appear in the literature each of which dealing with a different type of problem. In Fereira da Silva and Pereira Lopes (2006a; 2006b), the authors examine language variation in two distinct problems: (a) identification of whether a text is written in Portuguese or in a Brazilian dialect; (b) small touristic advertisements on the web, addressing foreigners but using local language to name most local entities. Their approach uses the Quadratic Discrimination Score to decide which cluster (language) must be assigned to the document they want to classify. Space properties of the clusters are based on a document similarity measure which is calculated using character n-grams. The authors conclude that discriminate elements depend on each specific context.

In Huges et al. (2006), the authors review a number of methods for enabling language identification in written language resources by focusing on cases such as: (a) the detection of the character encoding of a given document; (b) language identification for minority languages or unspecified language(s). They noticed that there is no one to one relation between a language and an encoding.

One of the most important papers on statistical language identification is presented by Dunning (1994). Dunning uses Markov Models to calculate the probability that a document originated from a given language model. In order to perform statistical language identification, a set of character level language models is prepared from training data during the first step. The second step involves the calculation of the probability that a document derives from one of the existing language models i.e., the probability that a String S occurs being from an alphabet X.

Another fundamental approach was proposed by Cavnar and Trenkle (1994). The authors calculated the N-gram profile of a document to be identified and compared it to language specific N-gram profiles. The language profile which has the smallest distance to their sample text N-gram profile indicates the language used.

A closely related work to ours is the one presented in Carter et al. (2011). In this work the authors introduce two semi-supervised priors to enhance performance at microblog post level: (i) blogger-based prior, using previous posts by the same blogger, and (ii) link-based prior, using the pages linked to from the post. The authors used the TextCat algorithm[1] and tested their models on five languages (Dutch, English, French, German, and Spanish), and a set of 1,000 tweets per language. Results showed that their priors improve accuracy but that there is still room for improvement.

Additionally, in the work presented in Winkelmolen and Mascardi (2011), the authors applied the well known Naive Bayes Classifier to perform language identification. The authors experimented on very short texts as well as on a corpus that they created from movie subtitles belonging to 22 different languages. To evaluate the impact of the use of different corpora, they compared the trigrams provided by TextCat with those obtained by their method. They concluded that a more accurate identification was obtained from their trigrams.

To the author's best knowledge, the only work that uses the notion of segmentation for the language identification task is presented in Zue and Hazen (1993), where a segment-based Automatic Language Identification (ALI) system has been developed. The system was designed around a formal probabilistic framework. The system incorporates different components which model the phonotactic, prosodic, and acoustic properties of the different languages used in the system. Practically the system investigates when an utterance should be segmented and how these segments can be characterized by a set of broad phonetic classes. The system was trained and tested using the OGI Multi-Language Telephone Speech Corpus. An overall system performance of 47.7% was achieved in identifying the language of test utterances.

The Greeklish phenomenon has been investigated in Chalamandaris et al. (2004), where the aim was to develop a module able to discriminate any Greeklish text from any other language. In order to surpass the problem of inconsistency in writing Greeklish, the authors made use of an alternative representation of every Greeklish word, namely a phonetic one. The performance of this module was tested with large multilingual corpora, where the initial Greek text was transliterated automatically according to four different sets of rules. The dataset consisted of: (a) public mailing lists; (b) private emails; (c) web pages in Greeklish written by more than 60 different persons in mixed Greeklish and English; (d) a large multilingual corpus whose content was varying from private and public emails, to web pages, newspapers, manuals, general documents, reports, and educational material for Greek high-school.

3 Method

In this paper we present an approach for language identification by using the technique of text segmentation. The text segmentation problem can be stated as follows: "*given a text which consists of several parts (each part corresponding to a different subject) it is required to find the boundaries between the parts*". In other words, the goal is to divide a text into homogeneous segments so that each segment corresponds to a particular subject while contiguous segments correspond to different subjects. In this manner, documents relevant to a query can be retrieved

[1] http://odur.let.rug.nl/~vannoord/ TextCat/

from a large database of unformatted (or loosely formatted) text. The problem appears often in information retrieval and text processing. One problem belonging to this category is language identification. To the author's best knowledge, it is the first time that text segmentation techniques are used to solve a language identification problem concerning text and not acoustic transcripts.

3.1 Text Segmentation Algorithms

The majority of text segmentation algorithms usually have as a starting point the calculation of the within segment similarity. This calculation is based on the assumption that parts of a text having similar vocabulary are likely to belong to a coherent topic segment. A significant difference between text segmentation methods is that some evaluate the similarity between all parts of a text, while others between adjacent parts. To penalize deviations from the expected segment length, several methods use the notion of "length model".

For our experiments we have chosen two well known topic change segmentation algorithms, the C99b implemented by Choi (2000; 2001) and the one proposed by Utiyama and Isahara (2001). Other algorithms presented in the literature proved to perform better in the Choi's benchmark corpus for the topic change segmentation task, such as the one implemented by Kehagias et al. (2004a; 2004b). However, the two selected algorithms benefit from the fact that they do not require training and their implementation is publicly available.

More specifically, Choi's C99b algorithm (2000; 2001) uses lexical cohesion as a mechanism to identify topic boundaries. This method uses the vector space model to projected words; sentences are then compared using the cosine similarity measure. Similarity values are used to build a similarity matrix. More recently, Choi improved C99b by using the Latent Semantic Analysis (LSA) achievements to reduce the size of the word vector space (Choi, 2001). Once the similarity matrix is calculated, an image ranking procedure is applied to obtain a rank matrix, which is a proportion of neighbors with lower values. The hypothesis is that LSA similarity values are more accurate than cosine ones.

Utiyama and Isahara (2001) propose a method that finds the optimal segmentation of a given text by defining a statistical model which calculates the probability of words belonging to a segment. Utiyama and Isahara's algorithm (2001) searches for segmentations with compact language models. The assumption here is that a segment is characterized by the distribution of words contained in it. Thus, different segments belonging to different topics have different word distributions. To find the maximum-probability segmentation, they calculate the minimum-cost segmentation by obtaining the minimum-cost path in a graph.

3.2 Corpus

As it was mentioned earlier, our work focuses on language identification on Greek forums. To the author's best knowledge, a publicly available corpus that examines the same problem does not appear in the literature. For this reason we created a corpus by collecting web pages taken from Greek university forums. The emphasis here was in collecting pages talking about a specific topic using Greek, Greeklish as well as English terminology. Thus, we collected 109 pages from the websites of the following institutions:

- University of Piraeus (28 pages)
- Technological Educational Institute of Athens (22 pages)
- National Technical University (NTUA) (3 pages)
- Aristotle University of Thessaloniki (69 pages)

Overall, our corpus consists of 17036 sentences, with the longest one containing 2582 characters. All the aforementioned web pages present strong variation in length as well as in the thematic category. In each of the aforementioned pages, an initial preprocessing was performed. Most specifically, sentences which were common or similar in each post, such as the post's theme (i.e, its subject), the date and time, the user login and other user's characteristics were removed. At a subsequent step, an annotation was performed where boundaries were placed at positions where the language used by the user changed.

Moreover, for English short function words such as prepositions, adverbs, adjectives as well as common verbs (e.g., the verbs "to be", "to have") in their variant forms were removed from the corpus. Additionally, stop word removal from a manually created list for Greek was performed. The stop list used for Greek is very similar to the one used for English. Stemming was also performed for English (i.e., substitution of a word by its root form) based on Porter's algorithm (Porter, 1980). Even though Greek is a heavily inflected language which means that a word may appear in many different forms, no further preprocessing (i.e., stemming and lemmatization) was performed for Greek.

Examination of the corpus led to interesting observations. A common observation is that users end their comments by the addition of a proverb as well as with facial expressions indicating their mood. However, in a number of cases, users writing their comment in Greek often finish their comment with an English proverb. On the contrary, users writing their comment in Greeklish often finish their comment with a Greek proverb. This makes the annotation (i.e., the choice of the boundary position) even harder because a boundary must be positioned before the proverb instead of being positioned at the end of user's post. Table 1 provides some examples of the different types combinations of comments and their corresponding proverbs written either using the same or using different languages for each pair comment-proverb of a post.

Another observation is the co-relation between the user's student identity and the language used. More specifically, we noticed that on the one hand, students belonging to technical departments choose to write their comments in Greek (but use a lot of technical terminology in English). On the other hand, the majority of law students write their comments in Greeklish. Users often start their comment in Greeklish and continue their post in Greek. Additionally, user's first word in the post corresponds to the login of the user to which they reply to. A frequent phenomenon is that users writing in Greek, also write English words using the Greek alphabet (for example, the word "thanks" is found as "θενκς"). Finally, emotional expressions are written in English (such as lol, evil, oops etc).

The purpose of the paper is the examination of whether a text segmentation algorithm is capable of identifying equivalent parts of text, where each part is written in different language. Since the topic in each web page of the corpus remains the same, the segmentation task here is to identify segment boundaries where each segment constitutes a text part written in Greek, or Greeklish, or English. Since text segmentation methods focus on sentence similarity or word distribution, the aim here is to identify where language changes according to the words appearing in a web page. In other corpora where language is common in all text parts, each segment corresponds to a different topic. In those contexts, change in word usage signals topic change and not language usage change.

4 Experiments

In this section we present the experiments we conducted to evaluate our method. We evaluate the application of a segmentation algorithm using the following three indices: Precision, Recall and Beeferman's Pk metric (Beeferman et al., 1997; Beeferman et al., 1999). Those metrics are commonly used in the text segmentation problem. Precision and Recall metrics are properly defined for the segmentation task. More specifically, Precision is defined as "*the number of the estimated segment boundaries which are actual segment boundaries*" divided by "*the number of the estimated segment boundaries*". Recall is defined as "*the number of the estimated segment boundaries which are actual segment boundaries*" divided by "*the number of the true segment boundaries*". The F measure which combines the results of Precision and Recall is not used here, due to the fact that both Precision and Recall penalize equally segment boundaries that are "close" to the actual i.e., true boundaries with those that are less close to the true boundary. For that reason, Beeferman proposed an new metric named Pk which measures segmentation *in*accuracy; intuitively, Beeferman's Pk measures the proportion of "*sentences which are wrongly predicted to belong to different segments (while actually they belong to the same segment)*" or "*sentences which are wrongly predicted to belong to the same segment (while actually they belong in different segments)*" (for a precise definition of Beeferman Pk metric see (Beeferman et al., 1997; Beeferman et al., 1999)). A variation of Beeferman's Pk metric, named WindowDiff index has been proposed by Pevzner and Hearst (2002). The WindowDiff metric remedies several problems of Beeferman's Pk and is also used in our evaluation. More specifically, the WindowDiff metric penalizes false positives and near misses equally. Since Beeferman's Pk and WindowDiff metrics measures segmentation *in*accuracy, low values of those metrics exhibit high performance of the algorithm examined.

Table 2 contains the obtained results after applying the two text segmentation algorithms in our corpus (where preprocessing has been performed as it was described in Section 3.2) using the four evaluation metrics described above.

Metric	Choi's algorithm	Utiyama & Isahara's algorithm
Precision	34.67%	23.88%
Recall	10.05%	62.35%
Pk	33.14%	46 %
WindowDiff	33.76%	62.9%

Table 2: Evaluation results

From the obtained results we can conclude that the segmentation accuracy differs from the one obtained in text segmentation corpora such as in Choi's benchmark (Choi, 2001). Choi's benchmark is used for text segmentation where the aim is to identify topic change. Reported results regarding Choi's benchmark can be found in Kehagias et al. (2004a; 2004b). It is worth mentioning that the aforementioned text segmentation algorithms are usually examined in problems where the number of segments, as well the number of sentences per segment do not exhibit strong variations.

In order to understand the obtained results, we calculated the minimum, maximum, and average number of segments as well the number of sentences per segment and their standard deviation. Table 3 contains the aforementioned statistics.

	Number of segments per document	Number of minimum sentences per segment	Number of maximum sentences per segment
Mininum	1	1	2
Maximun	428	11	402
Average	38,69	1,14	28,43
Standard deviation	49,54	0,989	28,18

Table 3: Statistics regarding the corpus

From the information listed in Table 3 we can see that our corpus presents strong heterogeneity as far as the number of segments per document and the number of sentences per segment are concerned. In other words, text segmentation for this corpus constitutes a difficult task, justifying the relative low performance obtained by the text segmentation algorithms.

The performance of the text segmentation algorithms presents strong interest. This is due to the fact that in traditional text segmentation corpora Choi's algorithm achieves lower performance compared to the one obtained by Utiyama and Isahara's algorithm. However, in the current problem the exact opposite phenomenon occurs. A possible explanation may be that Utiyama and Isahara's algorithm performs global optimization of a local cost function contrary to the local optimization of global information performed by Choi's algorithm. It may be possible that local optimization of global information may be more suitable for the nature of our corpus.

5 Conclusions - Future Work

In this paper we presented an attempt to perform language identification on a corpus which combines information written in Greek, English, and Greeklish using text segmentation algorithms. The novelty of our approach lies in the nature of our corpus as well as the use of this type of algorithms for the language identification task. Despite the difficulty of problem, we believe that the use of text segmentation algorithms constitutes a promising solution which however deserves further examination.

We outlook several directions of future work. The first direction considers the investigation of alternative segmentation algorithms.

The second considers comparison of our approach with other language identification tools. Arguably, the best known tool is van Noord's Text Cat, an implementation based on character n-gram sequences. Other well known implementations include BasisTech's Rosette Language Identifier[2] and a number of web based language identification services such as those created by Xerox[3] and Ceglowski[4]. Language::Ident is another interesting language identification tool [5] implemented by Michael Piotrowski. The program already comes with trained language models and so far supports 26 languages. Supported identification methods are N-grams, common words, and affixes.

A third direction of future work considers a more sophisticated preprocessing of Greek using a POS tagger and a lemmatizer such as the one developed by Orphanos (Orphanos and Christodoulakis, 1999; Orphanos and Tsalidis, 1999). Finally we consider the examination of other Greek corpora.

2 http://www.basistech.com/language-identifier/
3 http://open.xerox.com/Services/LanguageIdentifier.
4 http://search.cpan.org/~mceglows/Language-Guess-0.01/
5 http://search.cpan.org/~mpiotr/Lingua-Ident-1.7/Ident.pm

References

D. Beeferman, A. Berger, and J. Lafferty. 1999. Statistical models for text segmentation. *Machine Learning*, 34: 177-210.

D. Beeferman, A. Berger, and J. Lafferty. 1997. Text segmentation using exponential models. In *Proceedings of the 2nd Conference on Empirical Methods in Natural Language Processing*, 35-46.

S. Carter, E. Tsagkias, and W. Weerkamp. 2011. Semi-Supervised Priors for Microblog Language Identification. 2011. In *Dutch-Belgian Information Retrieval workshop (DIR 2011).*

W. B. Cavnar, and J.M. Trenkle. 1994. N-Gram-Based Text Categorization. In *Proceedings of SDAIR-94, 3rd Annual Symposium on Document Analysis and Information Retrieval.*

A. Chalamandaris, P. Tsiakoulis, S. Raptis, G. Giannopoulos, and G. Carayannis. 2004. Bypassing Greeklish!. In *Proceedings of LREC 2004: 4th International Conference on Language Resources And Evaluation. Lisbon, Portugal.*

F.Y.Y. Choi. 2000. Advances in domain independent linear text segmentation. In *Proceedings of the 1st Meeting of the North American Chapter of the Association for Computational Linguistics*, 26-33.

F.Y.Y. Choi, P. Wiemer-Hastings, and J. Moore. 2001. Latent semantic analysis for text segmentation. In *Proceedings of the 6th Conference on Empirical Methods in Natural Language Processing*, 109-117.

T. Dunning. 1994. *Statistical Identification of Language*. New Mexico State University. Technical Report MCCS 94-273.

J. Ferreira da Silva, and G. Pereira Lopes. 2006. Identification of Document Language is Not yet a Completely Solved Problem. In *Proceeding of the CIMCA '06 Proceedings of the International Conference on Computational Inteligence for Modelling Control and Automation and International Conference on Intelligent Agents Web Technologies and International Commerce.*

J. Ferreira da Silva, and G. Pereira Lopes. 2006. Identification of Document Language in Hard Contexts. In *SIGIR workshop on New Directions in Multilingual Information Access*, Seattle, USA.

B. Hughes, T. Baldwin, S. Bird, J. Nicholson, and A. Mackinlay. 2006. Reconsidering language identification for written language resources. In *Proceeding of the 5th International Conference on Language Resources and Evaluation (LREC 2006),* 485-488.

A. Kehagias, A. Nicolaou A., P. Fragkou, and V. Petridis. 2004. Text Segmentation by Product Partition Models and Dynamic Programming. *Mathematical and Computer Modeling*, 39: 209-217.

A. Kehagias, P. Fragkou, and V. Petridis. 2004. A Dynamic Programming Algorithm for Linear Text Segmentation. *Journal of Int. Information Systems*, 23: 179-197.

G. Orphanos, and D. Christodoulakis, D. 1999. Part-of-speech disambiguation and unknown word guessing with decision trees. In *Proceedings of EACL'99.*

G. Orphanos, and C. Tsalidis 1999. Combining handcrafted and corpus-acquired lexical knowledge into a morphosyntactic tagger. In *Proceedings of the 2nd Research Colloquium for Computational Linguistics in United Kingdom (CLUK).*

Porter, M.F. 1980. An algorithm for suffix stripping *Program*, 14(3) 130-137.

L. Pevzner, and M. Hearst. 2002. A critique and improvement of an evaluation metric for text segmentation. *Computational Linguistics*, 28(1):19–36.

M. Utiyama, and H. Isahara. 2001. A statistical model for domain - independent text segmentation. In *Proceedings of the 9th Conference of the European Chapter of the Association for Computational Linguistics*, 491-498.

F. Winkelmolen, and V. Mascardi. 2011. Statistical Language Identification of Short Texts. *In Proceedings of ICAART 2011 - Proceedings of the 3rd International Conference on Agents and Artificial Intelligence*, vol. 1-Artificial Intelligence, 498-503.

W. Zue and T.J. Hazen. 1993. Automatic Language Identification Using a Segment-Based Approach. In *Proceedings Eurospeech 1993*, 1303-1306.

Example	Message	Proverb	Case	Web page source
1	" καταρχας ειναι παρα πολυ σημαντικο που επιτελους ειδαμε και μια λυση πρακτικου!!!Αλλα Δημητρα μηπως σου ειναι ευκολο να "ανεβασεις" και το πρακτικο? Θα ηταν πολυ χρησιμο για εμας που το χρωσταμε...... Χαμόγελο Ευχαριστω εκ των προτερων.	*Go confidently in the direction of your dreams.... Live the life you have imagined*	Message in Greek, proverb in English	http://www.dapnomikis-thess.gr/forum/index.php?topic=54.0
2	Lacrimosa το συγκεκριμενο μαθημα ειναι λιγο δυσκολο. προσωπικα σαν μαθημα το βρηκα αρεκετα ενδιαφερον, αλλα αυτο ειναι προσωπικη εκτιμηση.	«Δε συμφωνώ ούτε με μια λέξη από όλα όσα λες, αλλά θα υπερασπίζω, και με το τίμημα της ζωής μου ακόμα, το δικαίωμά σου ελεύθερα να λες αυτά που πρεσβεύεις» Βολταίρος"	Both message and proverb in Greek	http://www.dapnomikis-thess.gr/forum/index.php?topic=54.0
3	se mia apegnwsmeni prospatheia na diavasw to sugkekrimeno ma8ima k meta apo polu kopo mporw na dilwsw oti : auto to ma8ima einai APAISIO!!!	"Be the change you want to see in the world!"	Message in Greeklish, proverb in English	http://www.dapnomikis-thess.gr/forum/index.php?topic=31.0
4	Dhmhtra nomizw pws to xe h tzwrtzakakh to a tmhma!ylh den poly yparxei pantws klassiko sos einai h athinaikh dhmokratia k h sparth me th gortyna na akolouthei ligo pio pisw.....	"Einai h palia froura pou epistrefei me fora...TO KANAME TOTE,MPOROUME KAI TWRA!!"	Both message and proverb in Greeklish	http://www.dapnomikis-thess.gr/forum/index.php?topic=31.0
5	einai kati simeiwseis gia to mathima dne kserw kata poso tha boithisoun alla elpizw...	ΗΡΘΕ Η ΩΡΑ ΤΗΣ ΑΝΑΤΡΟΠΗΣ...1η ΞΑΝΑ Η ΔΑΠ ΤΗΣ ΝΟΜΙΚΗΣ...	Message in Greeklish, proverb in Greek	http://www.dapnomikis-thess.gr/forum/index.php?topic=13.0

Table 1: List of examples of users comments and their corresponding proverbs

Lexicon induction and part-of-speech tagging of non-resourced languages without any bilingual resources

Yves Scherrer
Alpage, INRIA &
Université Paris 7 Diderot, Paris
yves.scherrer@inria.fr

Benoît Sagot
Alpage, INRIA &
Université Paris 7 Diderot, Paris
benoit.sagot@inria.fr

Abstract

We introduce a generic approach for transferring part-of-speech annotations from a resourced language to a non-resourced but etymologically close language. We first infer a bilingual lexicon between the two languages with methods based on character similarity, frequency similarity and context similarity. We then assign part-of-speech tags to these bilingual lexicon entries and annotate the remaining words on the basis of suffix analogy. We evaluate our approach on five language pairs of the Iberic peninsula, reaching up to 95% of precision on the lexicon induction task and up to 85% of tagging accuracy.

1 Introduction

Natural language processing for regional languages faces a certain number of challenges. First, the amount of electronically available written texts is small. Second, these data are most often not annotated, and spelling may not be standardized. One possible solution to these limitations lies in the use of an etymologically closely related language with more resources. However, in most such configurations, parallel corpora are not available since the languages are mutually intelligible and demand for translation is low.

In this paper, we present a generic approach for the transfer of part-of-speech (POS) annotations from a resourced language (RL) towards an etymologically closely related non-resourced language (NRL), without using any bilingual (i.e., parallel) data. We rely on two hypotheses. First, on the lexical level, the two languages share a lot of cognates, i.e., word pairs that are formally similar and that are translations of each other. Second, on the structural level, we admit that the word order of both languages is similar, and that the set of POS tags is identical. Thus, we suppose that the POS tag of one word can be transferred to its translational equivalent in the other language.

The proposed approach consists of two main steps. In the first step (Section 4), we induce a translation lexicon from monolingual corpora. This step relies on several methods, including a character-based statistical machine translation model to infer cognate pairs, and 3-gram and 4-gram contexts to infer additional word pairs on the basis of their contextual similarity. This step yields a list of $\langle w_{\mathrm{NRL}}, w_{\mathrm{RL}} \rangle$ pairs. In the second step (Section 5), the RL lexicon entries are annotated with POS tags with the help of an existing resource, and these annotations are transferred onto the corresponding NRL lexicon entries. We complete the resulting tag dictionary with heuristics based on suffix analogy. This results in a list of $\langle w_{\mathrm{NRL}}, t \rangle$ pairs, covering the whole NRL corpus. A more detailed overview of our approach is available in Figure 1.

We evaluate our methods on five language pairs of the Iberic peninsula, where Spanish and Portuguese play the role of RLs: Aragonese–Spanish, Asturian–Spanish, Catalan–Spanish, Galician–Spanish and Galician–Portuguese.

2 Related work

Koehn and Knight (2002) propose various methods for inferring translation lexicons using only monolingual data. They consider several clues, including the identity or formal similarity of words (i.e., borrowings and cognates), similarity of the contexts of occurrence, and similarity of the frequency of words. They evaluate their method on English–German noun pairs. Our work is partly inspired by this paper, but uses different combinations of clues as well as updated methods and algorithms, and extends the task to POS tagging. We shall now describe in more detail the three major types of clues used in the literature.

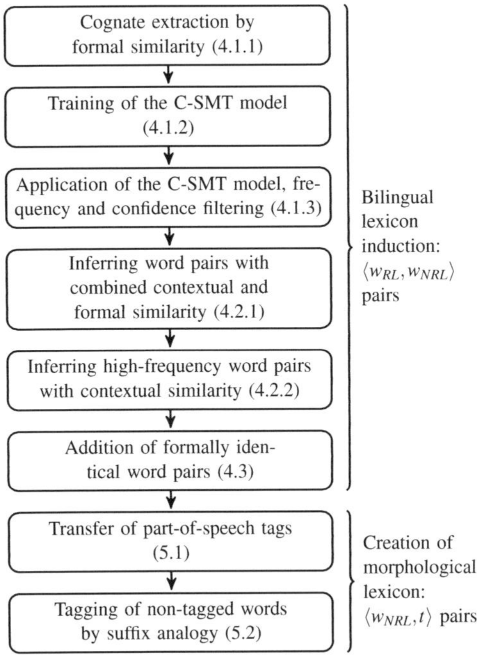

Figure 1: Flowchart of the proposed approach.

2.1 Cognate detection

Hauer and Kondrak (2011) define cognates as words of different languages that share a common linguistic origin. Two words form a cognate pair if they are (1) phonetically or graphemically similar, (2) semantically similar, and (3) if the phonetic or graphemic similarities are regular.

In closely related languages, cognates account for a large part of the lexicon. Mann and Yarowsky (2001) aim to detect cognate pairs in order to induce a translation lexicon. They evaluate different measures of phonetic or graphemic distance on this task. In particular, they distinguish static measures (independent of the language pair) from adaptive measures (adapted to the language pair by machine learning). Unsurprisingly, the authors observe better performances with the adaptive measures. However, they require a bilingual training corpus which we do not have at our disposal.

Kondrak and Dorr (2004) present a large number of language-independent distance measures in order to predict whether two drug names are confusable or not. Among the graphemic measures (they also propose measures operating on phonetic transcriptions), the BI-SIM algorithm (see Section 4.1.1) yields the best results. Inkpen et al. (2005) apply these measures to the task of cognate identification in related languages (English–French), and find that supervised classifiers do not perform better than language-independent methods with an accurately chosen threshold.

2.2 Character-based statistical machine translation

The principle underlying statistical machine translation (SMT) consists in learning alignments between pairs of words co-occurring in a parallel corpus. In phrase-based SMT, words may be grouped together to form so-called phrases (Koehn et al., 2003). Recently, a variant of this model has been proposed: character-based SMT, or henceforth C-SMT (Vilar et al., 2007; Tiedemann, 2009). In this paradigm, instead of aligning words (or word phrases) in a corpus consisting of sentences, one aligns characters (or segments of characters) in a corpus consisting of words. Of course, character alignments are well defined only for cognate pairs. Thus, it has been applied to translation between closely related languages (Vilar et al., 2007; Tiedemann, 2009) and to transliteration (Tiedemann and Nabende, 2009).

Whereas in the existing C-SMT literature training data is extracted from parallel corpora, we propose to create a (noisy) training corpus from monolingual corpora using cognate detection.

2.3 Context similarity

Exploiting context similarity is a promising approach for the induction of translation pairs from comparable corpora, whether the languages are closely related or not. The main idea (Fung, 1998; Rapp, 1999) is to extract word n-grams (or alternatively, bags of words) from both languages and induce word pairs that co-occur in the neighbourhood (context) of already known word pairs. For example, a French word appearing in the context of the word *école* is likely to be translated by an English word appearing in the context of the word *school*. This method requires a seed word lexicon (e.g., containing the pair $\langle$*école*, *school*$\rangle$), as well as large corpora in both languages in order to build sufficiently large similarity vectors.

Fišer and Ljubešić (2011) adapt this method to closely related languages: they build their seed lexicon with automatically extracted identical and similar words. Moreover, they take advantage of lemmatized and tagged corpora for both languages. Unfortunately, we lack annotated corpora for the non-resourced language — our goal is precisely to create such resources.

Context similarity methods have also been used in monolingual settings for lexical disambiguation (Bergsma et al., 2009) and for spelling correction (Xu et al., 2011): words that appear in similar contexts and are formally similar are likely to be alternative spellings of the same form. We pursue this idea in the area of closely related languages, where many word pairs not only are contextually similar, but formally as well.

2.4 Transfer of morphosyntactic annotations

The most straightforward idea for annotating a text from a non-resourced language consists in using a word-aligned parallel corpus, annotating the resourced side of it, and transferring the annotations to the aligned words in the other language. Yarowsky et al. (2001) successfully apply this approach to POS tagging, noun phrase chunking, named entity classification and even morphological analysis induction.

Another approach to this problem has been proposed by Feldman et al. (2006). They train a tagger on the resourced language and apply it to the non-resourced language, after some modifications to the tagging model. Such a tagger is bound to have a high OOV rate, and Feldman et al. (2006) propose two strategies to reduce it. First, they use a basic morphological analyzer for the non-resourced language to predict potential tags. Second, they extract a list of cognate pairs in order to transfer tags from one language to the other. While this approach looks promising, we chose to avoid the manual creation of a morphological analyzer, thus keeping our approach fully automatic.

3 Data

Our approach relies on three types of data:

1. A raw text of the NRL. From this text we extract word lists for cognate induction, frequency information by word-type as well as morphosyntactic contexts.

2. A raw text of the RL, from which we extract the same information.

3. A tag dictionary which associates RL words with their part-of-speech tags.

   We extract this dictionary from an annotated RL corpus; note however that tag dictionaries may be obtained from other sources, in which case no POS-annotated corpora are required at all by our approach.

Language	Sentences	Word tokens	Word types
Aragonese	335 091	5 478 092	215 809
Asturian	226 789	3 600 117	201 417
Galician	1 955 291	32 240 505	674 848
Catalan 200k	9 211	200 011	23 230
Catalan 500k	22 876	499 978	41 908
Catalan 1M	44 502	999 948	62 772
Catalan 10M	487 945	9 999 857	267 786
Catalan 50M	2 699 006	49 999 543	882 842
Catalan 140M	7 939 544	139 160 258	1 712 078
Spanish	23 381 287	431 884 456	3 451 532
Portuguese	12 611 706	197 515 193	2 252 337

Table 1: Wikipedia corpora

Language pair	Word types	Coverage
Aragonese–Spanish (AN–ES)	40 469	18.75%
Asturian–Spanish (AST–ES)	46 777	23.22%
Catalan–Spanish (CA–ES)	105 700	$\geq$ 6.17%
Galician–Spanish (GL–ES)	76 635	11.36%
Galician–Portuguese (GL–PT)	61 388	9.10%

Table 2: Size and coverage of the Apertium evaluation lexicons

The first two resources are used for the lexicon induction task, whereas the tag dictionary is required for the POS tagging task.

We test our approach on five language pairs: Aragonese–Spanish, Asturian–Spanish, Catalan–Spanish, Galician–Spanish and Galician–Portuguese, using raw text extracted from the respective Wikipedias. These language pairs vary widely in terms of available raw data and etymological distance, making them a good testing ground for our methods. Moreover, we use subsets of varying size of Catalan–Spanish to assess the impact of the data size (see Table 1).

We evaluate all five language pairs on the lexicon induction task on the basis of the dictionaries made available through the Apertium project (Forcada et al., 2011) (see Table 2).

The Spanish tag dictionary is extracted from the AnCora-ES corpus (Taulé et al., 2008).[1] It contains 42 part-of-speech tags and covers 40 148 words. The Portuguese tag dictionary is extracted from the CETEMPúblico corpus (Santos and Rocha, 2001).[2] It contains 117 part-of-speech tags (of which 48 are combinations of two tags) and covers 107 235 words.

[1] `http://clic.ub.edu/corpus/ancora` We have slightly modified the AnCora corpus to split multiword expressions and tag their components separately.

[2] `http://www.linguateca.pt/CETEMPublico/`

The Catalan–Spanish subsets are evaluated on the POS tagging task, using the AnCora-CA treebank as a gold standard. It is annotated according to the same guidelines as its Spanish counterpart.

4 Bilingual lexicon induction

In this section, we describe the different methods used for bilingual lexicon induction: the C-SMT method in Section 4.1, the n-gram context method in Section 4.2, and the addition of identical words in Section 4.3. Separate evaluations of the two former methods are presented in Sections 4.1.4 and 4.2.3 respectively.

4.1 Inferring cognate word pairs with character-based SMT

C-SMT models are generative models that translate words of the source language into their cognate equivalents in the target language. They are trained on a list of cognate word pairs, typically extracted form a word-aligned parallel corpus. Since we do not have bilingual data at our disposal, we propose to extract potential cognate pairs from two monolingual corpora (Section 4.1.1). Our hypothesis is that even with this noisy training data, the SMT models will learn useful generalizations. Section 4.1.2 describes the tools and parameters used for training the C-SMT model. Section 4.1.3 introduces two filters designed to further improve the precision of C-SMT.

For practical reasons, we infer the cognate pairs in the direction $w_{\mathrm{NRL}} \rightarrow w_{\mathrm{RL}}$, i.e., we consider the NRL as the source language and the RL as the target language. In particular, this allows us to match different w_{NRL} with the same w_{RL} and thus to take into account orthographic variation in the NRL. Such variation is less expected in the RL, which is assumed to have standardized spelling. Moreover, the classic SMT architecture puts the resource-intensive language model on the target language side, which is an additional argument in favour of the chosen translation direction.

4.1.1 Cognate extraction by formal similarity

We start by extracting word lists from the Wikipedia corpora. For the source language, we remove short words (<5 characters) and hapaxes. For the target language, we remove short words and words with less than 1000 occurrences.[3]

The formal similarity between two words is computed with the BI-SIM measure (Kondrak and Dorr, 2004). BI-SIM is a measure of graphemic similarity which uses character bigrams as basic units. It does not support swap operations, and it is normalized by the length of the longer string. Thus, it captures a certain degree of context sensitivity, avoids crossing alignments and favours associations between words of similar length. This measure is completely generic and does not presuppose any knowledge of the etymological relationship between the two languages. In contrast, it is not very precise and yields highly ambiguous results. For example, the Catalan–Spanish word pairs ⟨*activitat*, *actividad*⟩ and ⟨*activitat*, *activista*⟩ yield the same BI-SIM value, even if only the former can be considered a cognate pair.

For each source word w_{NRL}, we keep the $\langle w_{\mathrm{NRL}}, w_{\mathrm{RL}} \rangle$ pair(s) that maximize(s) the BI-SIM value, but only if this value is above the (empirically chosen) threshold of 0.8. This threshold allows us to remove unlikely correspondences. When several w_{NRL} are associated with the same w_{RL}, we keep all of them. The resulting list of cognate pairs is then used as training corpus for the C-SMT model.

4.1.2 Training of the C-SMT model

Our C-SMT model relies on the standard pipeline consisting of GIZA++ (Och and Ney, 2003) for character alignment, IRSTLM (Federico et al., 2008) for language modelling, and Moses (Koehn et al., 2007) for phrase extraction and decoding. These tools may be configured in various ways; we have tested a large set of parameter configurations in preliminary experiments, but due to space restrictions, we just mention the parameter settings that we finally retained.

- We add special symbols to the beginning and the end of each word.
- We train a character 10-gram language model on the target language words. We removed words appearing less than 10 times in the corpus; each word is repeated as many times as it appears in the corpus.
- GIZA++ produces distinct alignments in both directions. Among the proposed heuristics, the *grow-diag-final* algorithm was the most efficient.

[3]This threshold has been introduced to reduce the complexity of comparing every source word with every target word. We have found that a lower threshold does not necessarily improve the results.

	Source	BI-SIM		C-SMT		Frequency filter		Confidence filter	
	words	Recall	Precision	Recall	Precision	Recall	Precision	Recall	Precision
AN–ES	92 393	34.52%	64.44%	100%	76.26%	100%	74.45%	94.04%	74.54%
AST–ES	77 517	43.02%	62.76%		75.02%		74.93%	89.11%	78.50%
GL–ES	280 828	23.68%	41.26%		69.57%		72.20%	90.66%	72.85%
GL–PT	280 828	14.93%	36.83%		48.89%		53.06%	89.90%	53.31%
CA–ES 200k	8 781	57.18%	68.03%	100%	70.42%	100%	69.08%	83.07%	77.37%
CA–ES 500k	16 456	52.83%	64.26%		70.92%		69.81%	82.18%	78.31%
CA–ES 1M	25 633	47.36%	60.39%		69.86%		69.29%	81.56%	78.01%
CA–ES 10M	111 232	27.34%	45.01%		62.93%		65.55%	88.05%	69.09%
CA–ES 50M	363 627	16.81%	37.61%		56.13%		62.19%	90.28%	63.18%
CA–ES 140M	750 287	11.81%	34.94%		51.52%		58.41%	89.30%	59.13%

Table 3: Evaluation of the cognate word induction steps. Recall refers to the percentage of source words for which the respective method yielded at least one target word. Precision refers to the percentage of correct pairs among the answered pairs whose source word appears in the evaluation lexicon.

- We have disallowed distortion (i.e., the possibility of changing the order of characters) to avoid learning crossing alignments, which we suppose very rare in the context of word correspondences between related languages.
- *Good Turing discounting* is used to adjust the weights of rare alignments.
- The different parameter weights of an SMT model are usually estimated through *Minimum Error Rate Training* on a development corpus. However, the tuned weights yielded worse results than the default weights, due to the large amount of noise in the training data. Thus, we kept the default weights.

4.1.3 Application of the C-SMT model and filtering

Once trained, the C-SMT model is used to generate a target word for each source word, using the same list of source words as for the creation of the training corpus. This is thus a completely unsupervised approach. Now, the C-SMT model may also generate RL words that occur less than 1000 times and that have been filtered out during training.

In line with the findings of Koehn and Knight (2002), preliminary experiments have shown that word pairs with large frequency differences are often wrong. For example, Catalan *coneguda* 'known' is associated with Spanish *conseguida* 'reached' instead of the more frequent (and correct) *conocida* 'known'. Therefore, we generate a 50-best list of candidates with C-SMT and rerank them according to the frequency similarity between the source word and the target word. Frequency counts are extracted from the monolingual Wikipedia corpora. In the following, we refer to this as *frequency filtering*.

Moreover, the absolute C-SMT and frequency scores are a good indicator of the quality of the translation pair. These scores allow us thus to remove word pairs that are likely to be wrong, by adding a second filter. It eliminates all candidates whose combined score is less than 0.5 standard deviations below the mean of all combined scores. We call this *confidence filtering*.

4.1.4 Evaluation

Table 3 shows the results of the different lexicon induction steps described above.

Unsurprisingly, the training corpus extracted with the BI-SIM method is rather noisy, with precision values of less than 70%. Its recall values are low as well: target candidates were found only for 11% to 58% of the source words.

This picture changes impressively with the C-SMT model trained on these noisy data. Not only does it generate a candidate for each source word (recall of 100%), but the resulting precision values improve by about 10% absolute on average.

The frequency filter only seems to work reliably when the source language corpora are large enough (from the 10M Catalan subset onwards, and including Galician). The confidence filter improves precision values at the expense of recall; its relevance thus largely depends on the task at hand. Still, precision values are higher than 70% and recall values higher than 80% in most experiments.

Finally, one may note that, despite the filters, precision degrades drastically with very large source corpora (> 10M running words). This is likely to be caused by the addition of rare words, which are often named entities that do not follow the regular graphemic correspondences.

4.2 Inferring word pairs with contextual similarity

For several reasons, methods based on formal similarity alone are not always adequate: (1) even in closely related languages, not all word pairs are cognates; (2) high-frequency words are often related through irregular phonetic correspondences; (3) pairs of short words may just be too hard to predict on the basis of formal criteria alone; (4) formal similarity methods are prone to inducing false friends, i.e., words that are formally similar but are not translations of each other. For these types of words, we propose a different approach that relies on contextual similarity.

Suppose that our corpora contain the Catalan segment *diferència de càrrega elèctrica* and the Spanish segment *diferencia de carga eléctrica.* Suppose further that the C-SMT system has inferred the word pairs ⟨*diferència*, *diferencia*⟩ and ⟨*elèctrica*, *eléctrica*⟩. These word pairs allow us to match the two segments and to propose two new potential word pairs, ⟨*de*, *de*⟩ and ⟨*càrrega*, *carga*⟩. Other context pairs may then validate or invalidate these word pairs.

We use 3-gram context pairs of the type $\langle w_1 w_2 w_3, v_1 v_2 v_3 \rangle$, with already known word pairs $\langle w_1, v_1 \rangle$ and $\langle w_3, v_3 \rangle$, to infer the new word pair $\langle w_2, v_2 \rangle$. Likewise, we use 4-gram context pairs of the type $\langle w_1 w_2 w_3 w_4, v_1 v_2 v_3 v_4 \rangle$, with already known word pairs $\langle w_1, v_1 \rangle$ and $\langle w_4, v_4 \rangle$, to infer the new word pairs $\langle w_2, v_2 \rangle$ and $\langle w_3, v_3 \rangle$. We skip punctuation signs in the context construction.[4]

It is evident that word pairs inferred by matching contexts are extremely noisy. We therefore propose two filtering approaches: a filter based on both context frequency and formal similarity criteria for cognates and near-cognates (4.2.1), and a back-off filter based on frequency criteria alone for short high-frequency words (4.2.2).

[4]It is also possible to use a 3-gram context in one language and a 4-gram context in the other one to infer word pairs of the type $\langle w_2, v_2 v_3 \rangle$ or $\langle w_2 w_3, v_2 \rangle$. Such patterns are useful if the two languages have different tokenization rules. For example, they have allowed us to obtain the Asturian–Spanish pairs ⟨*a l'*, *al*⟩ and ⟨*polos*, *por los*⟩. However, for the time being, we have not integrated such asymetric alignments in the evaluation framework and in the POS tagging pipeline.

4.2.1 Combined contextual and formal similarity

We filter the $\langle w, v \rangle$ word pairs obtained by context matching according to the following criteria:

- Word pairs inferred by one single context are not deemed reliable enough.
- We also remove word pairs with a relative string edit distance higher than 0.5.[5]
- For a given source word, we remove all contextually inferred target candidates in the lower half of their frequency distribution and in the lower half of their distance distribution. This allows us to focus on those candidates that are clearly more similar than their concurrents.

A lot of the retained word pairs have already been proposed by the C-SMT method. We found that 70%-80% of the contextually inferred word translations are identical to the C-SMT translations, whereas 10%-20% of word pairs are new, and the remaining 5%-15% concern source words which were translated differently with C-SMT. Among this last category, we mainly find different inflected forms of the same lemma, and different transliterations of the same named entity. However, the context approach also corrects some erroneous C-SMT pairs, such as Aragonese–Spanish ⟨*charra*, *carrera*⟩ 'talks/race', replacing it by the correct ⟨*charra*, *habla*⟩. Therefore, when merging the C-SMT word pairs and the context word pairs, we give precedence to the latter.

4.2.2 Removing the formal similarity criterion for high-frequency words

The combined filter unfortunately removes some high-frequency grammatical words that are either non-cognates (e.g. Catalan–Spanish ⟨*amb*, *con*⟩), or whose forms are too short to compute a meaningful distance value (e.g. $\langle i, y \rangle$ with a relative edit distance of 1.0). For these cases, we introduce a back-off filter that lacks the formal similarity criterion and focuses only on frequency cues.

Concretely, each source word that has not obtained a target candidate with the previous approach is assigned the target word with the high-

[5]Since the contexts already constrain the potential word pairs, we chose to be more tolerant with the formal similarity criterion and explicitly use a lower threshold (0.5 instead of 0.8) and a simpler distance measure (string edit distance instead of BI-SIM) than above.

	Combined		High-frequency	
	Pairs	Precision	Pairs	Precision
AN–ES	3389	88.35%	35	34%
AST–ES	7549	92.56%	37	65%
GL–ES	22933	94.58%	91	67%
GL–PT	12518	87.04%	90	42%
CA–ES 200k	292	89.92%	7	40%
CA–ES 500k	915	94.77%	14	60%
CA–ES 1M	1676	94.80%	32	78%
CA–ES 10M	9065	94.03%	90	71%
CA–ES 50M	17014	92.96%	141	67%
CA–ES 140M	20514	91.87%	186	60%

Table 4: Evaluation of the word pairs induced by contextual similarity.

est number of common contexts, provided that this number is higher than 5.

Moreover, we have opted for a pigeonhole principle here: we disallow a target word to be matched with more than one source word. In our case, this prevents all pronouns to be assigned to the more frequent definite determiners.

This filter yields only a small number of word pairs, but they are of crucial importance since their token frequency is very high.

4.2.3 Evaluation

The performance of the context similarity approach is illustrated in Table 4.

The combined similarity method yields word pairs with very high precision. The number of induced word pairs grows according to the size of the corpus from which the contexts are extracted.

The high-frequency word approach works less well: the number of induced word pairs is very low, and translation precision falls drastically. While the quality of the word pairs induced with this approach may be insufficient for lexicon induction, we still deem it good enough for the POS tagging task. Indeed, the reliance on context similarity means that even if the induced word forms are wrong, they are still of the correct grammatical category. For example, the Galician–Spanish words $\langle \textit{boa}, \textit{gran} \rangle$ are not translations of each other but are both adjectives.

4.3 Addition of formally identical word pairs

Even after the application of the C-SMT and context lexicon induction methods, many words remain untranslated. (Remember that the recall figures of Table 3 refer to the number of source words used for this method, which excludes hapaxes and words with less than 5 characters.) For these words, we simply check whether they figure in identical form in the target language. This mainly allows us to add punctuation signs, but also abbreviations, numbers and proper nouns.

5 Creation of the morphological lexicon

In the preceding sections, we have described how we induce a bilingual lexicon from monolingual non-annotated texts. In this section, we use this lexicon to create a POS tag dictionary for the NRL, and use it to annotate texts.

5.1 Transfer of morphological annotations

The bilingual lexicon induced above contains $\langle w_{\text{NRL}}, w_{\text{RL}} \rangle$ pairs. Annotation transfer amounts to (1) loading an existing $\langle w_{\text{RL}}, t \rangle$ tag dictionary for the resourced language, and (2) merging these two resources by transitivity in order to obtain $\langle w_{\text{NRL}}, t \rangle$ pairs.

The tag dictionaries extracted from AnCora-ES (for Spanish) and from CETEMPúblico (for Portuguese) contain ambiguities, i.e. words that are assigned several part-of-speech tags depending on their syntactic function. For the time being, we do not deal with these ambiguities, but we rather associate each word unambiguously with its most frequent POS tag. With this simplification, merging the two dictionaries by transitivity is straightforward.

5.2 Adding morphological annotations by suffix analogy

At this point, there still remain untagged NRL words, either because no induced bilingual word pair contained it, or because the corresponding RL word was not found in the tag dictionary. In this case, we guess its tag by suffix analogy. We identify the longest suffix that is common to the non-annotated word and to at least one annotated word, and we transfer the POS tag of the annotated word to the non-annotated word. If several annotated words share the same suffix, we choose the most frequent POS tag.

5.3 Distribution of POS tag induction methods

Table 5 shows the percentage of word tokens and word types that have been tagged with the different tag induction methods. As already mentioned above, the C-SMT approach is mainly used for long low-frequency words that contain regular

	Tokens				Types			
	C-SMT	Context	Ident.	Suffix	C-SMT	Context	Ident.	Suffix
AN–ES	14.8%	49.1%	20.4%	15.7%	13.5%	1.6%	3.5%	81.4%
AST–ES	11.3%	54.2%	18.8%	15.7%	14.3%	3.6%	4.0%	78.2%
GL–ES	8.0%	59.1%	18.8%	14.1%	6.3%	2.6%	1.3%	89.8%
GL–PT	15.0%	55.2%	20.8%	9.0%	15.5%	2.2%	3.6%	78.7%
CA–ES 200k	17.7%	43.2%	20.5%	18.6%	14.8%	1.1%	16.9%	67.2%
CA–ES 500k	18.2%	47.9%	18.3%	15.6%	20.7%	3.0%	14.6%	61.7%
CA–ES 1M	17.4%	52.0%	17.2%	13.4%	24.4%	5.0%	12.9%	57.8%
CA–ES 10M	14.4%	62.3%	15.1%	8.3%	30.2%	16.3%	7.0%	46.5%
CA–ES 50M	14.2%	64.5%	14.1%	7.2%	29.3%	21.7%	5.4%	43.6%
CA–ES 140M	15.4%	63.5%	14.0%	7.1%	29.8%	21.8%	5.1%	43.4%

Table 5: Distribution of the origin of the induced POS tags, by word types and tokens.

phonetic correspondences. The contextual similarity methods are used for frequent words. The context methods account for more than half of the tokens, but for no more than 22% of the types. The *Identical* category mainly concerns punctuation signs, which again have high token frequencies. Finally, suffix analogy is used for the overwhelming majority of word types, but accounts for less than 20% of token frequencies.

The size of the source corpus impacts the distribution of the different tagging methods: the coverage of the context similarity methods increases, while the other methods are used less frequently.

5.4 Evaluation

Finally, we have evaluated the POS tagging accuracy of the Catalan–Spanish datasets, using AnCora-CA as a gold standard. The results range from 79.9% token accuracy with the smallest dataset up to 85.1% token accuracy with the largest one. All methods except suffix analogy yield accuracy rates higher than 70%. Given the difficulty of the task and the complete absence of annotated Catalan resources used in the process, these results can be considered satisfying.

As the corpus size increases, the highly accurate context similarity methods take over more and more words from C-SMT. For the remaining words, the C-SMT approach yields lower accuracy. However, this shift only has a small impact on the global accuracy rates, which seem to plateau at the 10M dataset. Adding more data above this threshold does not sensibly improve the results.

	C-SMT	Context	Ident.	Suffix	Total
200k	85.3%	91.7%	83.2%	43.3%	79.9%
500k	86.1%	91.1%	85.8%	45.2%	82.0%
1M	85.7%	90.4%	87.8%	46.9%	83.3%
10M	73.8%	90.8%	89.8%	51.2%	84.9%
50M	70.3%	90.0%	93.9%	52.3%	85.0%
140M	71.4%	90.1%	94.0%	53.6%	85.1%

Table 6: Token tagging accuracy on the Catalan–Spanish datasets.

6 Conclusion

We have proposed a combination of several lexicon induction methods for closely related languages and have used the resulting lexicon to transfer part-of-speech annotations from a resourced language to a non-resourced one. Note that this task is more complex than the more traditional task of non-supervised part-of-speech tagging, for which a POS dictionary of the respective language is generally available. We have applied our methodology to five Romance language pairs of the Iberic peninsula and evaluated it on different subsets of our Catalan–Spanish data.

Several aspects of this work may be improved. First, the assumed one-to-one correspondence between words and tags is clearly not satisfactory, and ambiguity should be introduced in a controlled way. This would also allow us to train a real POS tagger on the data, which could learn to disambiguate the words on the basis of the syntactic contexts and also tag unknown words more accurately than the suffix analogy method used here.

Second, we would like to replace the various threshold-based filters of the context similarity method by a more generic approach, possibly based on a classifier trained on the word pairs obtained with C-SMT. Unfortunately, first tests have resulted in insufficient recall.

Finally, we plan to validate our methodology on additional language pairs. We have started experimenting with Germanic and Slavic languages.

Acknowledgements

This work has been funded by the Labex EFL (ANR/CGI), operation LR2.2.

References

Shane Bergsma, Dekang Lin, and Randy Goebel. 2009. Web-scale n-gram models for lexical disambiguation. In *Proceedings of IJCAI 2009*, pages 1507–1512.

Marcello Federico, Nicola Bertoldi, and Mauro Cettolo. 2008. IRSTLM: an open source toolkit for handling large scale language models. In *Proceedings of Interspeech 2008*, Brisbane, Australie.

Anna Feldman, Jirka Hana, and Chris Brew. 2006. A cross-language approach to rapid creation of new morpho-syntactically annotated resources. In *Proceedings of the Fifth International Conference on Language Resources and Evaluation (LREC'06)*, pages 549–554.

Darja Fišer and Nikola Ljubešić. 2011. Bilingual lexicon extraction from comparable corpora for closely related languages. In *Proceedings of the International Conference on Recent Advances in Natural Language Processing (RANLP'11)*, pages 125–131.

Mikel L. Forcada, Mireia Ginestí-Rosell, Jacob Nordfalk, Jim O'Regan, Sergio Ortiz-Rojas, Juan Antonio Pérez-Ortiz, Felipe Sánchez-Martínez, Gema Ramírez-Sánchez, and Francis M. Tyers. 2011. Apertium: a free/open-source platform for rule-based machine translation. *Machine Translation*, 25(2):127–144.

Pascale Fung. 1998. A statistical view on bilingual lexicon extraction: from parallel corpora to non-parallel corpora. *Machine Translation and the Information Soup*, pages 1–17.

Bradley Hauer and Grzegorz Kondrak. 2011. Clustering semantically equivalent words into cognate sets in multilingual lists. In *Proceedings of the 5th International Joint Conference on Natural Language Processing (IJCNLP'11)*, pages 865–873, Chiang Mai, Thailand.

Diana Inkpen, Oana Frunza, and Grzegorz Kondrak. 2005. Automatic identification of cognates and false friends in French and English. In *Proceedings of the International Conference on Recent Advances in Natural Language Processing (RANLP'05)*, pages 251–257.

Philipp Koehn and Kevin Knight. 2002. Learning a translation lexicon from monolingual corpora. In *Proceedings of the ACL 2002 Workshop on Unsupervised Lexical Acquisition (SIGLEX 2002)*, pages 9–16, Philadelphia, PA.

Philipp Koehn, Franz Josef Och, and Daniel Marcu. 2003. Statistical phrase-based translation. In *Proceedings of the Conference of the North American Chapter of the Association for Computational Linguistics on Human Language Technology (NAACL-HLT'03)*, pages 48–54.

Philipp Koehn, Hieu Hoang, Alexandra Birch, Chris Callison-Burch, Marcello Federico, Nicola Bertoldi, Brooke Cowan, Wade Shen, Christine Moran, Richard Zens, Chris Dyer, Ondrej Bojar, Alexandra Constantin, and Evan Herbst. 2007. Moses: Open source toolkit for statistical machine translation. In *Proceedings of the 45th Annual Meeting of the Association for Computational Linguistics (ACL'07), demonstration session*, Prague, République tchèque.

Grzegorz Kondrak and Bonnie Dorr. 2004. Identification of confusable drug names: A new approach and evaluation methodology. In *In Proceedings of COLING 2004*, pages 952–958.

Gideon S. Mann and David Yarowsky. 2001. Multipath translation lexicon induction via bridge languages. In *Proceedings of the Second Meeting of the North American Chapter of the Association for Computational Linguistics (NAACL 2001)*, pages 151–158, Pittsburgh, PA, USA.

Franz Josef Och and Hermann Ney. 2003. A systematic comparison of various statistical alignment models. *Computational Linguistics*, 29(1):19–51.

Reinhard Rapp. 1999. Automatic identification of word translations from unrelated English and German corpora. In *Proceedings of the 37th Annual Meeting of the Association for Computational Linguistics (ACL'99)*, pages 519–526, Maryland, USA.

Diana Santos and Paulo Rocha. 2001. Evaluating CETEMPúblico, a free resource for Portuguese. In *Proceedings of ACL 2001*, pages 442–449.

Mariona Taulé, M. Antònia Martí, and Marta Recasens. 2008. Ancora: Multilevel annotated corpora for Catalan and Spanish. In *Proceedings of LREC 2008*.

Jörg Tiedemann and Peter Nabende. 2009. Translating transliterations. *International Journal of Computing and ICT Research*, 3(1):33–41. Special Issue of Selected Papers from the fifth international conference on computing and ICT Research (ICCIR 09), Kampala, Uganda.

Jörg Tiedemann. 2009. Character-based PSMT for closely related languages. In *Proceedings of the 13th Conference of the European Association for Machine Translation (EAMT 2009)*, pages 12 – 19, Barcelone.

David Vilar, Jan-Thorsten Peter, and Hermann Ney. 2007. Can we translate letters? In *Proceedings of the Second Workshop on Statistical Machine Translation*, pages 33–39, Prague, République tchèque.

Wei Xu, Joel Tetreault, Martin Chodorow, Ralph Grishman, and Le Zhao. 2011. Exploiting syntactic and distributional information for spelling correction with web-scale n-gram models. In *Proceedings of EMNLP 2011*, pages 1291–1300, Edinburgh.

David Yarowsky, Grace Ngai, and Richard Wicentowski. 2001. Inducing multilingual text analysis tools via robust projection across aligned corpora. In *Proceedings of the first international conference on Human language technology research*, San Diego, USA.

The Mysterious Letter J

Anđelka Zečević
Faculty of Mathematics
University of Belgrade
andjelkaz@matf.bg.ac.rs

Staša Vujičić Stanković
Faculty of Mathematics
University of Belgrade
stasa@matf.bg.ac.rs

Abstract

Ekavian and Ijekavian are two different variants of the contemporary standard Serbian language. The difference between them is related to the reflex of the old Slavic vowel *jat* and it influences both the speaking and writing language norms. The sensibility of existing language identification tools for both variants is of great importance for building representative corpora and development of relevant linguistics resources and tools underlying an automatic text processing. In this paper we present the results obtained after testing the three popular tools for language identification on corpora containing documents from each of the two variants. As it will be reported, the identification of Ijekavian variant is a much more difficult task since the observed tools are not adopted to it at all.

1 Introduction

The language identification is a problem of identifying the language a document is written in. It represents the fundamental step in tasks such as collecting the documents for corpora, machine translation and information retrieval. Because of its great importance, methodological approaches to the problem and submitted solutions are numerous. In the basis, the problem can be seen as a classification problem (Mitchell, 1997): if collections of known language samples represent classes, the problem of the language identification for the given document can be seen as a problem of the document assignment to the one of the classes in respect to relevant classification features.

Many sets of language features as well as classification algorithms have been tested so far. The choice of features might be linguistically motivated (diacritics and special characters) or more statistically oriented (word frequencies, n-grams of various lengths and types). The first tools were based on the analyses of character n-grams: Dunning (Dunning, 1994) introduced Markov models while Cavnar and Trenkle (Cavnar and Trenkle, 1994) worked with 1-NN classification algorithm. Nowadays the focus is on the diverse set of (dis)similarity measures (Singh, 2006) and powerful algorithms as can be read in papers discussing their performance and fields of the application (Martins and Silva, 2005).

The task of the language identification is considered much harder if the document is of modest length (for instance, e-Bay and Twitter messages or search engine queries) or the amount of available training data is limited. The same can be said for the cases when the number of considered languages is huge or languages are similar to each other. All these conditions influence the success rate as it is reported in Padró and Padró (Padró and Padró, 2004), Lui and Baldwin (Baldwin and Lui, 2010), and Milne et al. (Milne et al., 2012). We are especially interested in the latter problem since the Serbian language is closely related to the languages spoken in former Yugoslavia.

The standard Serbian language is formed on the basis of Ekavian and Ijekavian Neo-Štokavian South Slavic dialects and its form is determined by the reformer of the written language of the Serbs, Vuk Karadžić (1787-1864) (Stanojčić and Popović, 2011). In the common state of Yugoslavia this language was officially encompassed by Serbo-Croatian, a name that implied a linguistic unity with the Croats (and later with other nations whose languages were based on Neo-Štokavian dialects). In the last decade of the 20th century in Serbia the name

Serbo-Croatian was replaced in general usage by the name Serbian. As mentioned above, in Serbian speaking countries two dialects coexist. The Ekavian dialect is widespread in Serbia, while the Serbian Ijekavian dialect is presented in some parts of the northern Serbia, Croatia and Montenegro as well as Bosnia and Herzegovina. The difference among the dialects is related to the old Slavic vowel called *jat* and its conflation into the vowel *e* or diphthongs *ije* and *je*. It is notable in both spoken and written language forms as Serbian has a phonologically based orthography. For instance, in respect to the Ekavian dialect the English word *flower* has forms *cv**e**t* (long **e**) in nominative singular and *cv**e**tovi* (short **e**) in nominative plural while the appropriate forms in Ijekavian dialect are *cv**ije**t* and *cv**je**tovi* respectively. Therefore, Serbian and other languages of Štokavian provenance share the Ijekavian dialect in their standard forms which makes the task of the language identification very sensitive and error-prone. From the other point of view, these languages overlapping can help in cooperative development of tools and resources necessary for an automatic language processing (Vitas et al., 2011).

In this paper we present the results obtained after testing the three popular language identification tools on the collection containing both Ecavian and Ijekavian documents. Section 2 that refers to the related work and state-of-the-art approaches is followed by two introductory sections numbered as 3 and 4 and related to tested tools and specially created test corpora. The experiment is described in Section 5 while the results are presented in Section 6. The conclusions and ambitions for future work are summarized in Section 7.

2 Related Work

There is a number of papers discussing the identification of closely related languages, varieties of polycentric languages and language dialects. All these tasks are more advanced in comparison to classical ones and require application of more subtle techniques.

In the paper (Ljubešić et al., 2007) the three-phases model for differentiating Croatian from Slovenian and Serbian is presented. In the first phase the documents written in any of these three languages are singled out by the rule of 100 most frequent words and the rule of special character elimination. In the next phase character based second-order Markov model is developed aiming to distinguish languages among themselves. In order to improve the distinction between Croatian and Serbian, in the final phase the lists of forbidden words are introduced. Those are the lists containing words that appear in one language but not in others. The model is tested on the news collection and the achieved accuracy of 0.9918 is better than any reported for this group of languages.

The case of European and Brazilian Portuguese is discussed in (Zampieri and Gebre, 2012). As the differences between these two varieties can be described at orthographic, lexical and syntactic level, the identifying algorithm analyse three groups of features: character n-grams (n varying from 2 to 6), word unigrams and word bi-grams. The language models are calculated by using the Laplace probability distribution and evaluated on the journalistic corpora containing texts from the both varieties further classified according to their length in tokens. The achieved accuracies are 0.998 for 4-grams, 0.996 for word unigrams, and 0.912 for word bi-grams.

In order to identify Spanish varieties, the authors of (Zampieri et al., 2013) compared the classical character and word n-gram model to the knowledge-rich model based on the morphosyntactic information and parts of speech. The testing was done on the newspapers corpora from four Spanish speaking countries (Spain, Argentina, Mexico and Peru) and the reported results showed the direct relationship between the performance using these two language models: for instance, the Argentina-Spain classifier performed the worst in both cases (0.843 and 0.666 in terms of accuracy) while the Argentina-Mexico classifier generated the top results with characters and words (0.999) as well as morphology and parts of speech (0.801).

3 Tested Language Identification Tools

In our experiment we have tested three tools for the language identification. A brief description of tools and the motivation for the usage is given below.

Langid.py[1] is a top-level tool developed by Lui and Baldwin (Lui and Baldwin, 2012). It is based on the multinomial naive Bayes classifier which operates on the set of features (byte level unigrams, bigrams and trigrams) selected so that their information gain represents the characteristics of the language rather than the characteristics of the training domains (Lui and Baldwin, 2011). For the training phase the corpus, which encompasses government documents, newswire, online encyclopedia, software documentations and an internet crawl in 97 languages (Lui and Baldwin, 2011) is used. In the case of Serbian, the training collection includes XML wiki dumps for the period July-August 2010 as well as the set of manually translated content strings for a number of Debian software packages[2].

CLD (Content Language Detection)[3] is a library embedded in a Google's Chromium browser able to detect a language of a web page content. Thanks to Michael McCandless, it is singled out as a separated C++/Python module and ready for use on any UTF-8 encoded content. It is not specified how many languages it can detect (at least 76[4]) and so far it does not seem that the training set can be adapted to a specific usage.

The classifier developed by Tiedemann and Ljubešić (Tiedemann and Ljubešić, 2012) (in further text **Tiedemann&Ljubešić**) aims to distinguish closely related languages such as Serbian, Croatian and Bosnian. It is in the main multinomial Naive Bayes classifier trained over a parallel collection of news from Southeast Europe known as SETimes collection[5]. The usage of the parallel training set resulted in outperforming the state-of-the-art tools significantly since the data parallelism provided the same content and the focus on the differences among the languages. The authors also reported a list of the strongest discriminators among the observed languages and for our investigation it was interesting that the list for Bosnian contains many regular Serbian words in Ijekavian pronunciation (for instance, *izvještajima*, *posjetioci*, *djelimično*).

4 Test corpus

For testing purpose, we have created a corpus which consists of documents in both Ekavian and Ijekavian variant (Table 1). Since Serbian can be written in Cyrillic or Latin script, all the documents are transliterated into Latin script.

	Size (*in number of words*)	*Size* (*in MB*)
Ekavian part	2. 078, 172	13.2
Ijekavian part	528, 749	3.2

Table 1: The structure of the corpus

The Ekavian part of the corpus includes the articles from the daily newspaper *Politika*[6] for the years 2007 and 2010, the literary works written by the local authors and the translations of many popular novels. The list of all used materials is reported in Table 2.

The Ijekavian part of the corpus includes the articles from the daily newspaper *Glas Srpske*[7] for the period January-June 2013, some columns taken from the Deutsche Welle website [8] and famous works written in the Ijekavian dialect. Table 3 depicts all the details.

5 Experiment

Due to the nature of the used tools and comparability with other reported results, we have split the corpus into lines on average 400 words long. In the next step we have randomly selected 200 lines: the first 100 lines from the Ekavian part of the corpus and the rest from the Ijekavian part of the corpus.

For the testing purpose of the **langid.py** tool each line is saved as a separate file because a redirection mode was used. The **Tiedemann&Ljubešić** tool works with a single file that contains all the texts for classification as separate

[1] https://github.com/saffsd/langid.py

[2] In the time of writing this paper, translations in both Ekavian and Iekavian variants were available.

[3] http://code.google.com/p/chromium-compact-language-detector/

[4] http://blog.mikemccandless.com/2011/10/accuracy-and-performance-of-googles.html

[5] http://www.setimes.com

[6] http://www.politika.rs

[7] http://www.glassrpske.com/

[8] http://www.dw.de

[9] titles in Serbian are *Magareće godine* and *Glava u klancu, noge na vrancu*

[10] http://www.dw.de/škljocam-i-zvocam/a-4461937

Da Vinci Code by Dan Brown
1984 by George Orwell
Around the World in Eighty Days by Jules Verne
The Little Prince by Antoine de Saint Exupéry
The Diary of Anne Frank
The Hobbit by J. R. R. Tolkien
The Lord of the Rings by J. R. R. Tolkien
Solaris by Stanisław Lem
Winnie-the-Pooh by A. A. Milne
Bridget Jones's diary by Helen Fielding
For and Against Vuk by Meša Selimović
articles from *Politika* newspaper

Table 2: Ekavian part of the corpus

Springs of Ivan Galeb by Vladan Desnica
Selected works of Petar Kočić
two novels by Branko Ćopić[9]
Dove Hole by Jovan Radulović
Rebel and Rebel Janko by Simo Matavulj
Spiders and Searching the bread by Ivo Ćipiko
The Dervish and Death by Meša Selimović
articles from *Glas Srpske* newspaper
column written by Nenad Veličković [10]

Table 3: Ijekavian part of the corpus

lines so we concatenated our test lines into the document of this form. The same was done for the testing of **CLD** Python library.

6 Results

The obtained results are summarized in Table 4.

As it can be seen, the algorithms generally can cope with the classification of the documents in Serbian Ekavian variant (an average accuracy is 74.3%). On the contrary, the classification of the documents in Serbian Ijekavian variant is a very difficult task even for the tool developed with an idea of closely related languages in mind.

During the testing of **langid.py** tool we have encountered the problem with scripts: the tool by default recognizes Serbian only if it is written in official Cyrillic alphabet even though both Latin and Cyrillic alphabets are widespread in Serbian. This certainly caused the misclassification of all tested Ijekavian documents as Croatian.

Google's **CLD** obviously favors Croatian in both cases. In all the iterations the algorithm's confident parameter is set on the true value which means it is quite sure about the final outcome. After the analysis of the wrong results referring to Ekavian tests we found that in 25 iterations the second proposed language was Slovenian, in 8 iterations Serbian, and in 5 iterations Slovak. In all the remaining iterations the algorithm was completely sure about Croatian. In the case of Ijekavian tests, in 16 iterations the second proposed language was Slovenian, in 3 iterations Slovak and in 14 iterations Serbian. There was one iteration for each of the languages: Spanish, Italian and Indonesian.

The **Tiedemann&Ljubešić** tool is very accurate in classifying the documents in Serbian Ekavian variant while it recognizes a great part of Ijekavian documents as written in Bosnian. The latter is due to the fact that the training collection contains only the news in the Ekavian variant so the rules of Serbian are strictly learnt in this manner. In 83 of 98 iterations that output Bosnian as a result, the second proposed language was Croatian, and only in 15 of them it was Serbian.

7 Conclusions and Further Work

The obtained results show that many popular tools ignore the presence of the Ijekavian variant of Serbian language. This could lead to misclassification of Serbian documents which in turn strongly influences users' experience and information needs. The next steps would be enlarging the Ijekavian part of the corpus with relevant texts diverse in topic, genre and style and testing the observed tools on the training corpora extended with this part. In our opinion, this might alleviate the problem and help language identification algorithms learn both variants equally well.

8 Acknowledgment

This research was conducted through the projects 178006 and III 47003, financed by the Serbian Ministry of Science.

References

Timothy Baldwin and Marco Lui. 2010. Language identification: The long and the short of the matter. In *Human Language Technologies: The 2010 An-*

Tool		Serbian	Bosnian	Croatian	Other
langid.py	Ekavian	100	0	0	0
	Ijekavian	0	0	100	0
CLD	Ekavian	25	0	75	0
	Ijekavian	0	0	100	0
Tiedemann&Ljubešić	Ekavian	98	2	0	0
	Ijekavian	1	98	1	0

Table 4: The results

nual Conference of the North American Chapter of the ACL, pages 229–237.

William Cavnar and John Trenkle. 1994. N-gram based text clategorization. In *Proceedings of SDAIR-94, 3rd Annual Symposium on Document Analysis and Information Retrieval*, pages 161–175.

Ted Dunning. 1994. Statistical identification of language. Technical report.

Nikola Ljubešić, Nives Mikelić, and Damir Boras. 2007. Language identification: How to distinguish similar languages? In *Proceedings of the 29th International Conference on Information Technology Interfaces*, pages 541–546.

Marco Lui and Timothy Baldwin. 2011. Cross-domain feature selection for language identification. In *Proceedings of the 5th International Joint Conference on Natural Language Processing*, pages 553–561.

Marco Lui and Timothy Baldwin. 2012. langid.py: An off-the-shelf language identification tool. In *Proceedings of the 50th Annual Meeting of the Association for Computational Linguistics*, pages 25–30.

Bruno Martins and Mário J. Silva. 2005. Language identification in web pages. In *Proceedings of the 2005 ACM symposium on Applied computing, SAC'05*, pages 764–768.

Mary Milne, Richard O'Keefe, and Andrew Trotman. 2012. A study in language identification. In *Proceedings of ADCS'12*, pages 88–95.

Tom Mitchell. 1997. *Machine Learning*. McGraw-Hill.

Muntsa Padró and Lluís Padró. 2004. Comparing methods form language identification. pages 155–162.

Anil Kumar Singh. 2006. Study of some distance measures for language and encoding identification. In *Proceedings of ACL 2006 Workshop on Linguistic Distance*.

Živojin Stanojčić and Ljubomir Popović. 2011. *Grammar of the Serbian Language*. Institute for textbook publishing and teaching aids.

Jörg Tiedemann and Nikola Ljubešić. 2012. Efficient discrimination between closely related languages. In *Proceedings of COLING 2012*, pages 2619–2634.

Duško Vitas, Ljubomir Popović, Cvetana Krstev, Mladen Stanojević, and Ivan Obradović. 2011. *Languages in the European Information Society - Serbian*. Springer, Berlin.

Marcos Zampieri and Binyam Gebrekidan Gebre. 2012. Automatic identification of language varieties: The case of Portuguese. In *Proceedings of KONVENS2012*, pages 233–237.

Marcos Zampieri, Binyam Gebrekidan Gebre, and Sascha Diwersy. 2013. N-gram language models and POS distribution for the identification of Spanish varieties. In *Proceedings of TALN2013*, pages 580–587.

Author Index